Home and Back Again
My Journey Through
the Valley Of The Shadow Of Death

Home and Back Again
My Journey Through
the Valley Of The Shadow Of Death

Written by
Imelda Lorayna Fowler
with
Thomas E. Fowler

Copyright 2012

T X U 0 0 1 8 3 0 0 1 5

Rev. 1.1

Cover Design: T.E.Fowler

IMELDA   LORAYNA   FOWLER

Home and Back Again
My Journey Through
the Valley Of The Shadow Of Death

By
Imelda Lorayna Fowler
With
Thomas E. Fowler

This Book is Dedicated...

To our Loving Heavenly Father, who, because of His undying love for us, sacrificed His Son so that we can be redeemed and return to Him again. I thank Him.

To our Savior and King, the only Begotten Son of the Father, even Jesus Christ, whom I am eternally grateful that He gave His life for us that we may live again.

I KNOW He and the Father Lives for I have seen them!

To my eternal companion, Tommy, for his unconditional love and support. I love him so much!

To my wonderful children, Alona Joy (Southwick), and Raymond Boyd. Without a doubt, they are my greatest treasures! Thank you for blessing my life.

To our grandchildren, Emylee, Ethyn, and Eva, they are the most beautiful jewels I could ever have.

To my one and only son-in law, Bradley Dean Southwick, another gem of my life. Thank you for being part of our family.

Acknowledgements

This book would not be possible without the help of my brother-in-law, R. Merle Fowler who guided my husband and I through the process of outlining and developing each chapter.

My husband Tommy has labored intensively to help make this book a reality.

There are many friends and family who accepted the challenge of editing and re-editing the text.

Thank you all!

Home and Back Again
My Journey Through
The Valley Of The Shadow Of Death

Table of Contents

Introduction   9

Chapter 1   A Brief Summary Of My Childhood. 14
             A Belief In A Higher Power............. 16
             How I Met My Husband................... 20

Chapter 2   Coming To America......................... 25
             "Waves Of Joy" Alona Joy Is Born... 30
             Our Miracle "Bonus Baby"
             And My First Brush With Death....... 33

Chapter 3   A Family Desire Realized................. 38
             Power Lifting..................................... 41
             My Appendix Bursts......................... 44

Chapter 4   I See The Savior............................... 48

Chapter 5   My Brief Return... But Only
             For A Moment................................. 55
             The "Veil" Is Thin............................ 58
             Why Do "Bad" Things
             Happen To "Good" People?............... 60
             I Could Go Back If I Wanted............ 62
             A Terrible Vision Of The Future....... 64
             The Plain Of Hell............................. 65

My Visit Into The Garden.................. 67
The Power Of Thoughts –
An Out Of Body Experience.............. 69

Dying Can Be A Frustrating
Experience... 70

Chapter 6   The Pain Of Recovery....................... 73
"Babe, You've Got To
Get Some Sleep!"............................... 75
The Grand Council............................. 77

Chapter 7   An Encounter With The Adversary.... 83
The Importance Of Persistent
Prayer And The Devil's "Due Time".. 86

Chapter 8   I Finally Leave The Hospital............. 90
Another Out-Of-Body........................ 93
Here We Go Again!............................ 96

Chapter 9   My Recovery...................................... 98
Some New Spiritual Gifts Granted
To Others.. 99
My New Spiritual Gifts...................... 102
Mama Passes-On................................ 105

Chapter 10 Healing Hands and Hearts................. 109
The Most Powerful Force
In The Universe................................. 114

Introduction
by T.E. Fowler

When Dr. Raymond Moody released his groundbreaking book **Life After Life** in 1975, I was a junior in High School living in the small Southern California community of Ojai. I read and re-read the book with deep interest. I remember how taken back I was by the skeptical antagonism and sometimes angry defamation the book received from the Christian community. The Atheist religion, in its various forms, was set on its ear and even joined some Christians in their effort to vilify the book (strange bedfellows, eh?).

I could understand the terror a book like this could generate inside an atheist; for it fully exposes their fraud and rationalizations; their having put-off the Light Of Christ (that is given to every man, woman, and child) and the consequences of their deception, holds them up naked to the standard that they have forsaken – the belief and yes, the responsibility of accepting a Higher Power – God. For with that acceptance or denial comes the joy or sadness, freedom or bondage, obedience or defiance to His laws. These are the very laws (commandments) that govern the universe. I can only imagine the thought of having to face the full weight of disobedience to these universal laws and then standing before the Pure Loving Light of Jesus Christ to account for time wasted during this mortal testing ground. It is enough to make anyone frightened beyond imagination! It's no wonder that type of terror is called the "fear of the damned".

But why do Christians fear? When I read about the events brought forward in Dr. Moody's volume, the eternal part of me **knows** these things are absolutely true. That they took place and that similar events will be the "reward" of *all* men everywhere, of every religion, creed and color, is an inescapable, undeniable fact. The proof of countless witnesses all over the world is irrefutable. Then why shouldn't we Christians rejoice at this additional knowledge? We will have the opportunity to go into "the Light" and embrace He whose name we have professed and carried with us throughout our time on this earth. To be judged mercifully by the

Great Lawgiver, in perfect love and mildness for our faith and works done in this life – this will be our eternal reward! We will know first hand as they who have gone before us know, that His Grace is sufficient to save, even a vile sinner like me (and you).

Since Dr. Moody's book, dozens of other books and accounts have been published on the same subject, some personal and others from a more clinical point of view. I have studied most, if not all of them and will continue to do so for the rest of my life. I have also interviewed hundreds of persons who have "gone to the other side" and returned – forever changed. Although there are basic themes and similarities that coincide in nearly every Near Death Experience (NDE), it is the individual's *interpretation* of the NDE that almost always causes controversy. Thus, it remains up to the reader or interviewer to draw his or her own conclusions as to the meaning of why things took place slightly different or why one person's NDE was "deeper" than another's. We are left then to judge their beautiful, often sacred, sublime, and many times unspeakable, interaction with "The Light", using our own standard(s) of truth which we hold so dear and personal. I believe that we should never be critical of the experience itself, for it is sacred and special to the person who experienced it; but we should also reserve our opinions for the interpretation of what took place (and why) during their visit to the "other side".

A good example of this can be illustrated by interviewing children who have died and hence lived again. Because of their limited vocabulary and command of language, they can oft-times make some rather bizarre interpretations and observations (to a grown-ups way of thinking, anyway). Even eloquent adults will struggle for a label or a synonym to illustrate a place or an event in "heaven". We can turn to the Bible to see how the ancient prophets struggled to describe something as simple as modern day warfare, when they saw it taking place in visions several thousand years ago (for a good example see Joel 2:2-11 in the Old Testament). Words, labels, adjectives, mere written or spoken language simply cannot describe what wonderful places and relationships await us upon our return "home".

HOME & BACK AGAIN

It is for this reason, that I ask you to not be too critical of the events put forth in this small book. That they did happen is also an indisputable fact, for I was a witness to them. I sat in Medy's hospital room completely blown-away by what I was allowed to see and hear, as my lovely bride walked through "the valley of the shadow of death". Having studied these things for so long, I couldn't believe how fortunate I was to see them first hand (from a clinical standpoint anyway – on the other hand, my emotions were frazzled at witnessing my best friend "dying" several times).

When Medy approached me and asked me to write this book with her, we were both apprehensive. These experiences are extremely personal, but above all, they are *sacred* and casting them out before the world makes us both wary. Nevertheless, it is our desire that this book will give hope to the hopeless and strengthen those whose knees are weak and whose backs are burdened with the weighty things of this world. Above all, our hope is that this work will give to all individuals the desire to turn or return to Christ, the one and only true Light.

Our special thanks go out to my older brother Rick (R. Merle Fowler) who is an accomplished author of several masterfully written books. It is he who laid down the groundwork for this short volume.

So please, read and let the peaceable things of the Lord's Spirit interact with your "eternal" self – your spirit. We will leave the interpretation of the specifics to your standard(s) of truth. If there are errors, they are ours and we apologize beforehand for them.

Thomas (Tommy) E. Fowler

IMELDA   LORAYNA   FOWLER

Home and Back Again
My Journey Through
the Valley Of The Shadow Of Death

Medy Fowler October 1980

*Faith always implies the
disbelief of a lesser fact in favor of a greater.
A little mind often sees the unbelief,
without seeing the belief of a larger one.*

--- Oliver Wendell Holmes

Chapter I

A Brief Summary Of My Early Childhood

As a young girl growing up in the beautiful country of the Philippines, my father, Nemesio Lorayna was a principal of one of the local elementary schools in an outlying bario. He and my mother came from what we Americans would consider "humble" circumstances. However, Papa was brought-up to value an education even though obtaining one was not easy for him or his family. My mother, Emilia Marinda was the oldest of seven daughters (all very beautiful and full of life) and two sons. Her status as eldest meant she would not be allowed to graduate past the 6th grade, since her primary responsibility was to help her parents provide for her younger siblings. Still, she was a "catch" and Pa went to her parents to pre-arrange their marriage – a practice that is still the norm in some areas of the islands.

Nemesio and Emilia were married and started what was to become a large family. I am the youngest of 11 children. It may seem odd, but I have nieces and nephews that are my age and older! Indeed, we all grew up together on a rather large tract of land that my father had purchased surrounded by a thick, green banana plantation.

My childhood memories are a wonderful kaleidoscope of "sibling rivalries" and special play days with my nieces and nephews and a seemingly endless supply of cousins. Since Papa was a school principal and a local community leader, our neighbors watched our family carefully. As such, I was not allowed to get out of line very often. But because I was the youngest of so many children, many of the adults and my older brothers and sisters thought I was spoiled. Perhaps I was...

I worked hard in school and excelled in various leadership capacities. My teen years were fun and I have many happy memories associated with my youth. I *nearly* earned my degree in Foods and Nutrition from St. Thomas Aquinas University, until my husband proposed to me and cut my education short with just one semester left to graduate (the United States Fiancée Petition didn't allow for an extension).

It intrigues me as a (now) American, how many "first world" citizens look at my homeland of the Philippines as a poor "third world" country that has no running water and very little shelter for its people. Unfortunately, this is not an accurate assessment of my nation's culture and society. We Filipinos, as a nation, are a very industrious people producing legions of doctors, nurses, engineers, technicians and other professionals. In many ways, our educational standards are far better than those in America.

Agriculturally, the Philippines' rich volcanic soil produces so much food in abundance that, except in Manila where little food can be grown due to population density, starvation *was* unheard of. Sadly, since the U.N.'s introduction of the so-called Western Diet (refined, canned, processed foods), along with fast food chains and western style consumerism and blatant wantonness, our once thriving agricultural industry is now teetering. Farmers and their children have left their native homes for the bright lights of Manila in the hopes to reach the "gold paved streets" of America, Europe or Saudi Arabia. So now, in some places good farmland lays idle. We see similar problems happening in other island nations like Samoa and Tonga. Because of greed and poor forestry practices, beautiful rain forests are disappearing at an alarming rate. Once thriving ocean reefs are being wiped-out by desperate "fishermen" (they use arsenic and dynamite) to fill the growing need for tropical fish in saltwater tanks of "First World" countries. Also, previously unknown diseases like diabetes, chronic heart disease and cancer that were unheard of just a generation ago are now rampant.

Along with all that, the government encourages our brightest young minds to seek employment "abroad" (the largest and most profitable export of the Philippines is its people); so we have seen an interesting phenomenon known as "the great brain drain". Since we are the 3rd largest "English" speaking nation in the world, it appears many Filipinos are becoming the working class for the rest of the "First World". Tragically, the general health and vitality of my wonderful homeland and culture suffer in ways I never experienced during my childhood. But that rant is for another book.

A Belief In A Higher Power

While our family was large by any standard, we were basically a happy lot with Papa fulfilling his duty as a father and husband to his wife and ever increasing brood. Mama married Papa because, as I mentioned before, some of our island's Spanish tradition dictated an arranged marriage and was the accepted custom when a woman was betrothed to a man. Mama sometimes told me that she wasn't sure in the beginning if their relationship was going to work, but their love for one another showed as their family grew (and grew!) over the years. Since I was their last-born, I had a special relationship with my mother and father. I was the "Nene" (the youngest girl – pronounced Nee-nee) in the family and this allowed for some privileges as well as some disadvantages; like having to "share" anything and everything with my live-in female cousins and nieces, who were all my age.

We were practicing Catholics who followed the somewhat fanatical traditions of the Filipino people. All Saints Day or the "Day of the Dead" (in America we have the odd tradition of All Hollows Eve or Halloween); it was during this festive holiday when we would, as a community and a nation, celebrate and pray for our dead while elaborately decorating the cemetery in order to have a huge feast at the grave-site, to remember our departed loved ones.

HOME & BACK AGAIN

During Easter season, we would celebrate our week long mass or Passion, in which we would participate with other neighborhood families in staying up all night to recite written prayers. Of course, we small children would grow fidgety and tired during those all night prayer marathons and my Mama, grandma and aunties would smack the slackers as they nodded-off with a small switch made out of the inside of a coconut branch (they'd leave a nice welt!). The men spent those days and nights outside smoking and drinking. Since I was the Nene, I was allowed to sleep on my mothers lap during all the ruckus and commotion. No wonder they thought I was spoiled. I was!

These and other spiritual rituals and customs had a great impact on me as I got older. They laid a solid foundation of spiritual roots and a love for my Lord Jesus Christ that I am able to draw upon to this day. How grateful I am for the Catholic Church and my father and mother for those lessons they taught me, both in word and in deed.

Papa was not only a well-known local civic leader, but also he was a member of the prestigious Order of the Knights of Columbus within the Catholic Church and although that seemed like a big deal to me as a child, it was really my Mama who was the spiritual leader in our family. She taught me how to pray both vocally and in my heart. This deeply instilled in me the importance of turning to a Higher Power that, through our faith, could be summoned by diligent prayer. I feel fortunate to have learned early in my life that this effort to call upon God could sustain me through any difficulties.

Since we were already practicing Christians in the strictest sense, my belief in the Savior was prominent in my early childhood. I understood what "sin" was as it related to doing "bad" behaviors or thinking "bad" thoughts. I also began to realize just how important living a good, Christian life was and would continue to be as I got older and hopefully wiser.

When I became eight years old, I had my "First Communion" and it was an important rite-of-passage for me. Mama and Papa taught us the importance of having a one-on-one

17

confession of our sins. The emphasis in our lives was on faith and in doing "good", not only to others, but also to ourselves. There was very little debate or rationalization like there is today; as to what was "good" and to what was "bad". We knew if our heart told us it was bad, then it was and we did our best to avoid it. If it was good, we "sought after those things".

I remember during my childhood, Pa had a serious cataract condition that if not treated would cost him his eyesight. For a professional teacher and principal the consequences would have been disastrous. I remember our prayers of faith being focused on this, as we heard that an eye specialist from America named Dr. Carvajal was to visit our region for a short period. Our prayers were focused on our father being allowed to become one of his patients. The doctor was so busy and it just didn't seem possible for him to see Pa; but our prayers were finally answered and he had the cataract surgery. Although Papa would have to wear funny looking "coke bottle" glasses for the rest of his life, we felt that the operation was a complete success. For me, it was an extraordinary manifestation of the power of faith and prayers.

As a funny side story to my Papa's surgery, my Great Auntie Cipriana took me along with her to visit Papa during his recuperation in the hospital. She was visiting my family and purchased a small piglet from Mama. They put the unruly piggy into a rice sack for safekeeping. Foolishly, she gave me charge over the wriggling, squealing "package". While we were visiting in the hospital, I tried to sneak a peek at the cute black porcine in the sack. Suddenly the piglet jumped out of the bag and started running all over the hospital! Pandemonium! Like a slap-stick scene out of a cheesy old comedy; there I was, a little girl chasing a squealing, screaming pig (through a hospital!), under beds and occasionally knocking over carts, running down the hallways and in and out of stranger's rooms with my ancient Auntie bringing up the rear screaming at me louder than the pig! While all this time the doctor's, nurses and patients vainly tried to barricade the scampering bacon.

Can you imagine this same scene happening in USC Medical

today and the frivolous lawsuits and the "needed" legislation that would result? In the Philippines, it was just another day and it was all too funny. Although at that moment I was terrified of the repercussions I'd receive from my angry Aunt. Gratefully, I don't remember it being too bad. I was, after-all, the Nene.

A few months later my grandmother, the one with the really long prayers, passed away while I was still a little girl. This was a sad day for all of us, but it would help me to understand that death is indeed a part of life. In the Philippines back then, people were *born at home* and people *died at home*.

My other grandfather from my mother's side would often take cacao nuts and gather them up to make a special treat in which all of us children were involved. Papay (Grandpapa) would pick the pinkish cacao fruit and split it with his knife, exposing the white nuts inside. It was the children's job to extract the seeds and suck off the outer casing. The taste was "acquired", but not unpleasant. We'd then spit the large seeds into a bamboo basket (a winow-wind) where he would wash and then dry them in the sun. Soon after, Papay would roast the "beans" over an open fire and grind them (like coffee). The resulting powder was raw bitter chocolate, which we would eat on special occasions. Because cacao is a seasonal fruit, we savored these chocolate harvests and they were something we children looked forward to every year.

Raw Cacao Fruit

That's part of the reason why, when he passed-away in 1975; his loss was another real blow to the family. But by the time that had happened, my understanding of life and death had evolved and matured to the point that grieving and sadness was only a small part of my emotions.

Once, my mother told me that just before her father had passed away – while he was on his deathbed – he would often ask her for his shoes. She would reply that he no longer needed them. With that, he would *insist* that he had spent the past several hours walking a very long distance and that he was tired. While breathing very hard, like a runner who had just finished completing a marathon, he would lay there telling her that he had just got back from a long walk in a beautiful place full of flowers and that he now needed his shoes to complete the journey.

When she told this story to me, I somehow knew in my heart that what he said was actually true. He *had* taken a long walk, somehow. Although it seemed improbable, it was very real to him and my mother. His appendix infection ultimately cost him his life. Little did I know then how much impact his experience would have on me while I suffered through a similar ailment.

Sadly, most of us are led to believe that when someone dies, that is the end and we will never see him or her again. Death is an unspoken variable, a grand mystery, nothingness, a void that even our most devout priests weren't comfortable discussing. It was in these experiences and others that my faith led me to believe that there *had* to be more to living than just dying. The Lord must have some kind of grand purpose for all our existence. There must be something beyond...

How I Met My Husband

Leaving home to go to America has always been a dream for many. This includes those who live in far off places like Europe or other countries in Asia. For most of my peers and many other Filipinos, the U.S. is a kind of unreachable Nirvana. *Arizona Highways* magazine makes it all look so perfect, unblemished and beautiful. During my teen years, our region in the islands just got TV and although my family never bought a television, there were a few in our town who indulged themselves in the "reality" of shows like *Dallas, Dynasty* and *Falcon's Crest*. I never fell into that way of thinking.

Because of TV's portrayal of "America", so many Filipinos believed that in the U.S. *everyone* lived in large mansions with exotic cars parked in the driveway – there was no crime, no poverty, no flies and any problem could be solved in ½ an hour. When they looked around their (our) neighborhood, they saw ugly palm thatched houses often with dirt floors. They were upset by not having running water. They wanted to have servants go shopping for them and take care of their children (just like on T.V.).

Unlike so many of my peers, I saw the amazing, yet simple beauty of my homeland. I loved the neat little nipa huts (thatch houses) that lined our streets, alleys and walkways. Early every morning on my way to school, I could see all the Nene's sweeping their dirt pathways in order to keep them neat and tidy. Everywhere you go, you can hear the laughter of children, the cluck-cluck of chickens and the crow of roosters. Walking home on a warm moonlit night, you might hear a guitar and the soft singing of a young man serenading his girlfriend. Perhaps you'll see a tree full of alitaptap (fire flies), which is pure magic to behold. It is *always* so green and warm in the Philippines. Food is forever plentiful. You can pick mangos, bananas, guavas, papayas and other delicious fruit that grow wild everywhere. Walking to the market with my Mama was always fun, even when I was a teenager. We had a wonderful little house that was surrounded by fruit trees; children and chickens were everywhere. We had a small "piggery" where we raised and sold pigs to our neighbors and family. We had clean, fresh, cool water that we hand pumped from the family compound's well that was close-by in our back yard. Our house was the hub and I lived in the middle of all my older siblings and their numerous children. I loved attending school and going to church activities.

No, America and other places "abroad" had little pull or appeal to me. I'm sure had I remained and lived my life there, I would have been just as happy as I am now. In fact, Tommy and I are hoping to return and live there someday.

Many young girls in High School have aspirations to become registered nurses with the lofty goal to go abroad. Since I come from a family of teachers, it was assumed that I would follow the family vocation. I had other ideas. Mama wanted me to go to a trade school where many of my older siblings had gone. I didn't know it then, but I am extremely competitive and I believe that I could do *anything* that anybody else could do. Perhaps not for the same motivation, but I just need to know for myself that I could do it, too.

I took the nurses exam and passed, but my mother knew better. She knew for example, that I have a weak stomach for nefarious odors that most nurses have to face on a minute-by-minute basis. It was when I went to the hospital as a teenager and a potential nurse that I got a taste of reality; as the stench (that only hospitals have) coupled with elderly patients and their problems, woke me up to what that job really implied.

Mama was right and she guided me in another direction, where I pursued my Bachelors of Science in Foods and Nutrition.

Medy Graduating From High School

HOME & BACK AGAIN

Christian missionaries are a common occurrence throughout the world and the distant countries of South East Asia and the far-flung islands of the Pacific are no exceptions. A missionary is usually called to these remote places to not only help the poor and needy, but also to preach the Gospel of Repentance. Little did I know that my future husband would be one of those rare, selfless individuals who would spend his time and his own money to do just that.

He was serving in my small town of Daraga where he had been assigned with three other missionaries. It's funny to think about his 6' 3" stature and at over 180 pounds, we Filipinos thought he was John The Baptist resurrected! It's easy to picture him looking like some huge white giant among the short brown people of my island nation. He, and all the "Kanos" (Americans) were easy to spot not only because of their height and skin color, but also with their white shirts and ties, they really stuck out.

I first met him in front of our small church meetinghouse during November of 1978. Now don't think for a minute that I was "smitten" by him, for I wrote in my journal that fateful day:

"I met the new missionary today. His name is Elder Fowler, from California. *He's not really so very handsome...*"

We still laugh about that one! Well, you know what they say about first impressions. Working with the children at church, I found myself in front of the meetinghouse where I formally met Elder Fowler. A couple of years later, *after* we were married, he told me that he wasn't particularly impressed one way or another with me, because, after all, he was focused on missionary work and not on hustling a Filipina. He said that to him, I was just another "sister" who he had the opportunity to work with. I would occasionally see him while he served in Daraga; as my sister, Pilar and I would work together with him and his companions. This allowed some time over the next six months for us to interact, as we got to know one another on a spiritual, if not superficial level.

He was later transferred to the Northern Philippines where he would honorably finish out his two-year mission. It wasn't until he returned to his home in California that Elder Fowler (Tommy) proposed to me through a letter. Remember, this was done way before instantaneous electronic communication via the Internet was even thought of. E-mail was still at least another twenty years in the coming.

In that letter, we both agreed that on a certain day in the future, we would both set aside a specific time to fast and pray concerning our spending eternity together as husband and wife. We knew that this would be *the* most important decision we'd make in this lifetime and we wanted Divine guidance in the process. I followed the instructions by having a personal fast and intense prayer session by myself for that purpose at the same time he did 8,000 miles away. Soon after we wrote each other verifying that he/she was *the* one...

Lloyd's of London will insure almost anything
under the sun – including the weather!
But even Lloyd's of London will not insure
the success of a marriage! They will insure a ship on a
twenty-five thousand mile journey around the world.
They will not insure a marriage over a twelve-month
journey. The richest values of life are never mathematical,
they are moral ventures.

--- Professor Luccock

Chapter 2

Coming To America

The letters between Tommy and I continued as we jumped through all the bizarre hoops we call *legal* immigration. Even though we now had a Spiritual confirmation that we were to be married, the reality of that actually occurring seemed a long, long way off (read government red tape). Indeed, it took over nine months(!) before I was allowed to even speak to the American Consulate in order to get clearance to come to the U.S.A.

By the time everything was a "go", I was given only 90 days to fly to the States and get married (hence, I was unable to finish my last semester of college). If there is one thing my husband and I learned early on in our relationship is patience; *patience* in waiting on the Hand Of The Divine, *patience* when enduring through "unfair" problems, *patience* in allowing Satan his "due time", *patience* in the sure knowledge that *someday* we would prevail.

Our patience paid-off and on September 23, 1980 I boarded a plane with a small suitcase of personal possessions, leaving my family and friends – the only life I had ever known – to go to a cold strange place, full of weird foods, a bunch of white people and their backwards customs. It was a bittersweet moment saying goodbye to my wonderful parents, brothers, sisters, close friends and cousins. A few weeks later on October 2, 1980 Tommy and I were married in Oakland, California.

There were some funny moments of my arrival and consequent adjustments to a totally new way of life and lifestyle. For instance;

Tommy, as he puts it, was "goofy" with excitement when he came to pick me up at the San Francisco Airport (you could only imagine!). Although it seemed a little awkward for both of us in the beginning – remember, the last time we saw each other, he *was still* a missionary. However, we soon got over that and we began the process of getting to know each other on a more personal level. Since we both agreed to "save ourselves" until after we were married (we didn't even kiss each other until "over the altar"), getting to know one another was neither embarrassing nor difficult. We were just so happy and excited to finally begin this path we had chosen together that would ultimately take us throughout time and all eternity.

He felt he just "wanted to show me everything". So our first "romantic" dinner together was at the Burger King where the 680 and 80 freeways meet in Fairfield, California. I suppose I should mention here that Tommy is a lifelong surfer and he has chosen (by economic mandate) to make his (soon to be "our") lifestyle as simple (read cheap) as possible. So for our first dinner together, we sat down to: (2) Whoppers, (2) fries and (1) chocolate shake for me (I am after all special) and (1) DP for him (to keep him awake on the 3 hour drive back up to Paradise, California). I had never eaten anything like this before (where's the rice!?!?). I don't even like bread! I took one nibble on the burger (Tommy ate the rest and he has been gaining weight ever since!), I *sort of* liked the French fries but I *loved* that chocolate shake (one out of three isn't too bad).

Our drive home that night was just fun. Both of us were giddy in love, I think they called it "twitterpated" in Bambi. And twitterpated we were! His (our) car was an orange, 1977 SR-5 Toyota pickup with bucket seats. Since it was late September and starting to get very cold (at least for me), we had the heater up full-

26

blast. To this day, over 32 years (!) later, the battle over the car heater still rages. I have been able to adjust to everything American, except the cold. Tommy can still be sweating while I'll be freezing at the same time, and so it was that first anticipation filled night.

On that drive up the state throughout the evening, we passed skunk after rancid skunk. There are no skunks in the islands, so I had never smelled anything like this before and I THOUGHT IT WAS TOMMY "CUTTING LOOSE"! Instead of plugging our noses at noxious smells like Americans do, we Filipinos are more subtle and simply put our index finger under our nose to show our distaste. Of course for his part, he just smelled another dead skunk. After a while and after several skunk stations into our journey, Tommy noticed my finger under my nose and he also noticed me backing as far into the corner of that tiny Toyota cab as I could. It was about this time that I was wondering just what I had gotten myself into; was I about to marry a man with the worst smelling farts possible? Why didn't anyone warn me!?!? Once he knew what was going on, he tried in vain to explain that it was just a "small animal" that was making the awful stench. "Sure", thought I, "that's what my Papa used to say too, but even *his* never smelled *that* bad..." It wasn't until he showed me a ran-over animal and I took in the "full effect" of the pungent perfume at point-blank range that I actually believed and forgave him. Phew! I was able to breathe a cautious sigh of relief.

Tommy had rented a very small house for our first home (it was once a log cabin that he was refinishing the interior in exchange for rent); I was going to stay with his parents and younger brother Jimmy (19 years old) and their little sister Beri (14 years old) for the next two weeks. What fun we all had together! His family was so excited to finally meet me. They showed me so much love and like Tommy, they "wanted to show me everything". It was their love for me, along with the fact that I knew this is what the Lord wanted me to do, which helped ease the pangs of homesickness.

Even though it was very late in the growing season, Dad took me outside the next morning to pick and eat fresh strawberries that still grew in good numbers (Tommy's dad, was an excellent "gentleman farmer"). I also was able to pick apples right off the trees (!) – this was something I had always dreamed of. I didn't bring many warm clothes (there are none in the Philippines); so the church members were more than happy to fix me up with an abundance of their pre-teen daughters clothing (I'm only 4'10" and weigh about 92 pounds). I was given a Bridal Shower, wherein I met so many of my soon-to-be dear friends in Paradise, California.

Medy & Tommy Newlyweds 1980

HOME & BACK AGAIN

My brother-in-law Jimmy makes the best salsa and he couldn't wait to "guinea pig" the new Filipina. I unknowingly took a whole tablespoon full and promptly vomited it all back up! What an embarrassing mess! Up until then, I never really knew how bland Filipino food was, as we don't "spice-up" our food like Latin cultures do; so when I got a whole mouthful of albeit *mild* chili, my stomach revolted. It was an awkward moment for both Jimmy and I that we laugh about today.

During my first pregnancy, I got to where I couldn't stand to be *near* any Mexican food. Poor Tommy, he loves the stuff and occasionally he'd try to sneak in a taco or burrito for lunch while at work. Four hours later, I could still smell the lingering aroma (as only a pregnant woman can) and I knew immediately he had "cheated" on me. I would banish him to the bathroom where he would penitently brush his teeth for several minutes as part of his repentance. Only then would I allow him to get his "honey I'm home" kiss.

Thankfully, I've since learned to love and embrace Mexican food (and culture) and have also learned my brother-in-law's secret to creating a truly masterful salsa.

Tommy's little sister Beri was in constant amusement with my behavior for those first few years (she and I still laugh a lot together). We had no phones in the Philippines back then (we had to go to the phone company to make a call), so for me, making even a simple call was a totally new learning experience. One day while still living at my in-laws, I tried to dial my only relative living in the U.S. and I had miss-dialed the number. Of course the PacBell female computer recording came on, only I didn't know it was a recording. I got very angry at Ma Bell for constantly repeating the same thing over and over again! What, did she think I was stupid? I didn't know I could just hang-up to make it all stop, but not wanting to offend, I thought it might be rude to just cut her off. When Beri came over to investigate and discovered whom it was I was "talking to"; she busted out in laughter (much to my embarrassment – she has a really loud cackle). It seemed everyday, every situation was going to be a learning moment for me.

My mother-in-law is a gifted seamstress and she did a masterful job in sewing my wedding dress. After we got married, I moved into the cabin. Tommy and Jimmy did their best to make it a comfortable home for us. It was. Water beds were "the thing" back then and we had a huge one that nearly took up the entire cabin! Even though I turned the heater up full-blast, I still froze my little brown butt off every night while my poor husband spent the night lying on top of the blankets sweating (love is a powerful thing!).

Before we were married, Tommy and a friend started a fledgling microcomputer company that did okay, but he had problems with his partner and decided to leave. This was during what he calls the "Jimmy Carter" recession in the early 80's; so finding computer work was not always easy for him. But he was young and a hard worker and since his pre-mission occupation was General Contracting, he was *barely* able to keep us going doing concrete finishing, carpentry, carpet laying and any other "labor" jobs he could muster-up. Fortunately, he had learned to trouble shoot, program and even build computers while he was a partner in his previous business; so his skills have been able to evolve and he has made a satisfactory career in the IT business throughout our lives.

"Waves Of Joy"; Alona Joy Is Born

Tommy took a "temp" job for Northrop King Seeds and it required our moving to Chico, just down the hill from Paradise – in all, we've moved over 20 times in the 32 plus years we've been married. It was a fun time for us that next summer, even though I was very pregnant. His job allowed us to travel all over Northern California and to save money, we brought along our tent and sleeping bags. My husband loves to travel and I was soon hooked as well. The biggest problem for him living in Chico/Paradise, as beautiful as they are with all the pine trees and rivers (he loves to fish); they are still so far from the ocean. As I've mentioned before, he is a hard-core surfer and living away from the beach was difficult for him. With this job he was able to explore and go surfing in the cold, remote reaches of the "North Coast".

By the time his contract with NK was finished just before Christmas 1981, I was 9 months along and I felt I was ready to burst! On the night of the 22nd, my water broke. We were both so young and inexperienced; we thought I had just had "an accident" (even though I never had one before). About 3:00 AM early the next morning, Tommy called his mother because I was now "cramping" real bad. "You Bozo, she's in labor! Get her to the hospital, NOW!" was her less than gentle reply.

My now very nervous husband gently helped me into our little truck and the three of us headed up to Paradise. In just a couple *seemingly* very long and intense hours later, we met Alona Joy (Waves of Joy) for the first time. She had a very full, thick head of hair. As a matter of fact, her whole body was covered in little black hairs. Beri said she looked like a little brown monkey. She also had large black eyes and sometimes when I'd dress her up, she looked like a little "China Doll". How beautiful she was! How happy we all were together.

Alona's birth seemed like such a natural, biological part of being married and since Tommy and I decided that we'd let the Lord give us as many children as He wanted; we just assumed we'd be blessed with a large family (Tommy's parents have 8 kids, my parents have 11). Heavenly Father saw it differently. Even though we had hoped for more like her, Alona was to be an only child for nearly 17 years.

IMELDA LORAYNA FOWLER

Alona Joy at 8 months

Tommy got a good contract working on Arco Oil's computers way up in Prudoe Bay, Alaska. The trouble was he worked six-week tours with only two weeks off. Yes, the money was very good, but it was really tough on all three of us. We tried to remedy the situation by moving me and the baby up to Alaska (in the middle of winter). You can imagine how that went.

Baby and I went to live with my Aunt and her large family of boys (6) in Livermore, California. It worked out well for all, since the boys ranged from ages 9 years to one month older than Alona; I was able to take care of the boys while Mama Diths and Papa Joe worked at their busy schedules. When Tommy would come home for his two weeks off, we'd spend the time surfing in Ventura, where he grew-up. Still, neither of us was happy with the arrangement.

We spent the next several years moving around and working in places where my husband could contract computer work. For 7½ years we lived in Crescent City when he got a great job working for Del Norte County's computer department. He also worked a second job as a radio DJ (hardly a job, but a fantasy for him). My education paid-off and I became employed by the Del Norte Senior Center as the Nutrition Director. What a delightful job that was!

I love working with older people. It was fun to meet such a diverse and interesting group. Some of them had strong feelings of racial bigotry (unfortunately, that was sometimes a part of that older generation) and I had to win them over with love and kindness. And win them over I did! When I left the Senior Center seven years later, I didn't feel one bit of prejudice or bigotry from even the most grizzled old codgers who gave me nothing but grief when I started. In fact, they all became my dear friends whom I look forward to seeing again in the next life.

If you are a young person reading this (younger than 50), I strongly suggest you take some time and volunteer in any capacity with our senior citizens. It is most rewarding to just sit and listen to them share their life's experiences. When someone is in the "sunset" of their lives, they feel an overpowering urgency to "teach" what they've learned to a younger person. Your time spent together will help them to fulfill that need and you will gain the wisdom and valuable insight from their "living history". Senior citizens are a group of people who have truly "been-there-done-that".

Our Miracle "Bonus Baby" And My First Brush With Death

We had a wonderful time in Crescent City, but my husband's stress level was at maximum. His Dad had passed-away a few years earlier at a young 64 years old, of heart failure. Then soon after, Tom's just older brother Bob died of a heart attack at the very young age of 38. It seems his family has a genetic heart defect that sadly has also affected him – when he, too, had a heart attack at age 38. However, unlike his brother, Tommy quit his job and made recovering his health a priority.

Of course, the consequences of quitting a job for any reason can be dire. "Dire" hardly tells the story. We lost *everything* except our love for one another. Cars were repossessed, etc. But Tommy's still alive and doing quite well, thank you very much.

Alona was a beautiful young teen now and had had a very successful career as a swimmer while we lived in Crescent City. She even set several pool swim meet records throughout Northern California and Southern Oregon that still stand today.

Beri invited us to come live with her back in Chico at her best friend's large ranch (we call Marianne our adopted sister). All went well while Tommy rehabilitated. He was able to get a job delivering brand-new motor homes for Fleetwood. It was a fun job with little stress and littler money. But at that time our financial stability wasn't nearly as important as his health.

It was during this phase that an amazing thing happened; I was pregnant! Well, we thought I was anyway. I had what is called a Molar Pregnancy, which is to say when the egg divided; it just kept dividing into a large mass (not a fetus). Although I was showing all the symptoms of a normal pregnancy, this type of mass is potentially cancerous. My doctor gave me several drugs, but they made me so sick I was unable to move or breathe easily. I felt as weak as a newborn kitten and I knew my life was in danger. Many women who have had complications while giving birth know the feeling. They can sense their life *ebbing* away, not in a drug induced sort of way, but a very real sensation that their body will not be able to support their spirit to keep them alive any longer. All that bleeding causes the very essence of their existence to somehow *flow* out of them. In my heart I knew that if *I* didn't change things, I would not be able to survive.

The above statement is not a knock against doctors or modern drugs. It is to say that I've been given wrong, even harmful drugs and diagnosis by "practicing" professionals before and, as we will see soon, later in my life. My warning to all is simply to not put *all* your trust and faith in so-called modern medicine and too many of its proponents who arrogantly dismiss any other alternatives as "quack" medicine.

Like Tommy's heart condition, we decided to go the "holistic " route. We are blessed in that we have a few friends who are gifted naturopaths – skeptics call them "Witchdoctors" – we call them healers. I was given an herbal regiment that removed the entire tumor within a couple of weeks with no side effects.

It was just before I started my herbal process, when I was literally bleeding to death, that my spirit left my body. It's odd, but the sensation of "dying" is nothing short of *natural*. Certainly it is as normal an event as is birth, sans the pain. It felt as natural as could be; all pain had ceased and I felt *free*. There I was floating above my body looking down at my self, when suddenly I realized what was taking place. Could this actually be happening? Was it really "my time" to go? I thought of my beautiful teenage daughter and my loving husband and felt sad, because I knew they would miss me. But there was a feeling inside of me that told me it was *not* my time to leave. I knew that was true and as I caught hold of that sentiment, my body jumped as I took a deep breath and *my spirit was sucked back in through my chest*! Suddenly I was in severe pain again, although more intense and more real than ever before.

The whole Molar Pregnancy incident shook all three of us to the core. Like any disaster or near disaster, it came as something "out of the blue". You cannot plan for it; you cannot anticipate all future health problems or anything like it. People who try are usually neurotic pessimists who are completely unhappy in life. Anyway, such negative thinking is the total opposite of my overly optimistic nature.

While we continued to stay at my sister-in-law's home for several more months, Alona had a vivid dream. In that dream a *young man* came to her and said he was her brother (she felt like she'd known him forever) and that he was now ready to come to earth.

Not too long after her dream, I once again started showing signs of being pregnant. I get really, really sick when I'm prego. After the previous episode we were still skeptical and a bit nervous. However, when the "home test" showed "2 lines", I knew I had to ask my Heavenly Father what this was all about. While I was in deep prayer, my mind had a vivid vision of a small boy with wonderful big brown eyes and a thick head of dark hair. He had a "bowl" hair cut and looked like a real life version of Walt Disney's Mobley, in the Jungle Book. In the apparition he was joyfully playing with me and around me. With that vision in my heart, I knew nothing less than a miracle was about to burst into our simple lives.

A friend asked us to house sit while they were away for several months. The house was on the coast in Fort Bragg, California, so we jumped at the chance to move back to the beach. During that time, Tommy was asked to help a couple deliver their yacht to Southern California and that would give us some much needed income. With me very pregnant, he asked how I felt about it. I knew I'd be fine (Alona was now 16 and was able to look after my needs) so I gave him the green light. He made it back just a few days before little Ray-Ray made his appearance.

Since the time Alona was born and all the intervening years; we'd hoped for another child. But unlike Alona, who although was and is still very special to us, her conception and birth just seemed like part of the natural biological process of what happens when a man and a woman are married. The process (not the child) can easily be taken for granted. Raymond (who is named after my noble father-in-law) on the other hand came to us after 15 plus years of hope and then a near disaster. To say that he is nothing short of a miracle is still an understatement.

Through the whole natural process, we continued to learn patience in waiting on the hand of the Lord. Truly, He is in charge and in times when you and I are feeling alone and life is playing "unfair" games; we can rest assured that these things are allowed to "buff-off the rough spots" and make us more *humble* and *meek*. After all, it is "the meek" who will "inherit the earth".

Alona's College Graduation – Raymond, 1 Year Old

And so the stream of life that flows out from the altar of
sacrifice in the temple of the human soul,
will bring life and joy and beauty to human hearts
all along the way.

--- H. S. Putnam

Chapter 3

A Family Desire Realized

One winter evening, while we lived in Crescent City, Tommy broached a question to me that after a while really took root in my heart. As I mentioned before, he loves to travel and now *we* love to travel. We like meeting new people and visiting new (to us) places. Sampling strange foods is always interesting. Most importantly though, we love the closeness it brings our little family when we drive long distances together. The problems we have in our lives seem so distant when compared to the excitement we feel while driving to see family or to visit old haunts.

Here was his proposal: "Perhaps we could purchase a small yacht (a *boat* by "yacht" standards), live on her for a while and learn to sail while we pay it off and fix it up. Then we could sail her to the Philippines via Mexico and the South Pacific." For leverage on that cold, rainy Crescent City night; he added, "we'll be sailing through the tropics the entire time..."

"The *tropics* you say... hummmm..."

We bought a 25-foot boat (now that *is* small!), put most of our worldly possessions in storage and moved aboard her. Alona was about 9 years old then and we also had our small sheltie dog, "Jaws". It was an exciting time in our lives. What fun we had during the 3 plus years while we lived and sailed on *Our Moon*.

Alona, Jaws, Medy, Tommy on "Our Moon"

Tragically, after Tommy's heart attack, we lost pretty much everything. We had just purchased a new (to us) 35-foot sailing ketch that we had hoped to sail across the Pacific. How heartbreaking it was to sign the foreclosure papers. We were able to keep *Our Moon* and we moved her to Lake Oroville, near Beri's place in Chico. Thankfully that helped us continue to keep "the dream" alive while we sailed her around the lake every chance we got.

After moving to Fort Bragg, my husband's recuperation was nearly complete and he was able to find a good job in Willits, California, where he managed the computers of a small mail order/Internet company. We sold *Our Moon* and her trailer to finance our move back to the coast. All this happened soon after Raymond came to us.

Our sailing dream now had one major issue; our then home of Willits, albeit closer to the ocean than was Chico, was still too far away to both live on a boat and work at his present job. The commute, although beautiful, was hard on our cars and way too expensive. We needed a solution.

Our nation was now beginning to see an expanding "bubble" in the housing market (of course we all know what ultimately happened to that bubble). After months of studying, I passed the California Department of Real Estate Exam and went to work hoping to earn enough money to put down on another boat and sail it to the Philippines.

The housing market in Southern California was exploding, so Tommy quit his job and we moved down to the land of traffic, attitude and smog. Unfortunately, along with the aggressive housing activity, the yacht market was also experiencing a boom. So finding a good boat at a price we could afford was nearly impossible. Still, we persevered and found a lovely 35-foot ketch in Long Beach that fit our needs – even though we were to learn after it was too late that her motor was frozen solid – "welded", Tommy said.

Still, we were happy to be back on the water. Sadly for us, Alona by now had long since moved away and was on her own. Ray-Ray wasn't three years old yet, so we put netting on the lifelines and laid-down an *unbreakable* law that he had to wear his life jacket whenever he left the cabin. He soon got to where he NEVER went outside without his preserver on. We loved being back aboard on the water, but more importantly; we loved the fact that we were moving back towards our sailing dream.

Family Portrait – Raymond 2 ½ years old

Power Lifting

When I came to America I couldn't do even *one* sit up. Not that I was overweight or anything like that; but rather, like all Filipinas from my generation, I never had the need to do any form of *formal* exercise. Tommy on the other hand was a "gym rat" and started lifting weights when he was 15 or 16 years old. He had always hoped we'd be "workout partners" together. Like most women, I mistakenly feared lifting weights would make me look like the steroid freak-show bodybuilders on ESPN. Despite his constant encouragement and prodding, I resisted.

Then one day I injured my shoulder badly while at work. Our holistic doctor/friend was also an avid lifter in the gym Tommy trained in. His prescribed therapy was light resistance training

41

(weight lifting). Because it was a "treatment", not *really* lifting, my husband finally got me into the gym.

As time went on, I soon realized that I really enjoyed the feeling lifting weights gave me. Before this time, I had become a strong advocate of aerobic workouts on VHF video and participated daily; but this weight lifting stuff, gave me a whole new feeling of empowerment that I've never experienced before. It was during my "therapy" when I became Tommy's workout partner. One day while we were doing a "back routine", my partner/trainer set up an Olympic barbell with 135 pounds (that's two large 45 pound "plates" and the bar). He showed me the proper technique to dead-lift (lifting the weight up from the ground to your waist) and let me give it a go. To my utter astonishment the weight popped right up! He added a couple "dimes". 155 pounds went up just as easily! Then finally **185 pounds**! This was my first time ever doing the deadlift. At the time I weighed about 89 pounds. My trainer said, "Cool... Do it again". I did, but this time for three reps!

Two months later we entered me in the California "Novice" Power Lifting meet, in San Jose. I won my weight class and beat all the other heavier women. To everyone's surprise (including the judges), I won the Overall Lifter – including the men (they use a body weight-to-strength formula). Who'da thunk-it?

For the next several years, I would compete throughout the Western U.S. and once at the National Finals in Dallas, Texas where I took a third over-all. I was able to set several California and Nevada state records. Last time I looked on-line, I was still in the Women's Top 20 All-Time 97 pound class (that's the lightest weight class) World Record Holders. To me this means a lot, because so many of the lifters today holding records – male and female – are European and Chinese, where steroids are used regularly. Then as well as today, I lift completely "drug-free". My best totals are:

Squat: 285 lbs. Squatting in competition means bringing your butt below your knees. Tommy calls them a "low-bar" squat.

Deadlift: 336 lbs. From the floor to your waist. I use "sumo" style.

Bench Press: 120 lbs. My long arms keep me from performing a strong bench.

Total Combined Weight: 741 lbs. It is the *combined weight* that the "formula" is used to determine the overall-lifter.

It's always fun to go to these meets. When we walk in together, everyone assumes it's my massive husband with his 56" chest & 21" arms who will be doing the competition. Imagine their surprise when all 4' 10" and 92 pounds of raw-brown Filipina steps-up on the platform. Imagine their disbelief when I sometimes walk away with the Overall Lifter trophy!

Life was good for us, we continued to train together and although our boat motor was a welded basket case, we were still happy to be living on the water. We home school Raymond and just enjoy spending as much time with him as we could. In all, we were happy and we felt blessed in every facet of our lives.

A few trophies from the early days.

My Appendix Bursts

On Sunday, July 4th, 2004, we had just come home from church when I began to experience stomach flu-like symptoms. As the week wore on, I just felt sicker and the pain was becoming extreme; my fever hit the roof. Some of my friends were saying I might be having appendicitis – others didn't think so because I "wasn't in enough pain". I should mention here that I seem to have an above normal tolerance for pain – and as my husband and family will attest, I'm not usually one to complain about bodily discomfort. Regardless, I was hurting more than anything I'd previously experienced in my entire life – even more than having a baby! On the following Thursday, at about 7:00 PM we unwillingly went into the local hospital emergency room.

The "emergency" check-in procedure took SEVERAL HOURS!!! I've often wondered if we had good insurance if it would have only taken 10 minutes? When they reluctantly admitted me, I sat until midnight and then I finally got into the x-ray room. I was still in extreme pain and was given nothing but mild oral pain pills (our own).

I was asked and then checked by a very nice nurse to see if I was pregnant. Unfortunately, I knew I was not.

A while later a young intern came into my room to inform me, no, I was not pregnant (duh!) and then went on to study my "film". He *quickly* glanced at it and said he "could find nothing unusual" about my scan. "You probably have severe flu or a 'mild' case of food poisoning, perhaps a gall-stone?" And with that he left the room and I never saw him or another doctor the rest of that fateful night.

An administrative nurse came in and asked me if I had made out my "last will" and would I like to donate any of my organs? "Yes I would", I retorted in a smart-aleck way "I would like to donate my appendix!" She could feel my frustration.

The Filipino MRI Technician, who knew how to read the scan better than the "doctor", saw what was happening and had overheard the medical staff saying they wanted to transfer me to a County Hospital three hours away. He came to me in secret (probably at the peril of his job) and whispered to me in Tagalog (Pilipino), "Tell your husband to not let them transfer you... it is your right to refuse this... **don't let them move you**... you'll never survive the trip..." He then left the room.

My poor tired and bewildered husband was *allowed* to come into the room a few minutes later. I weakly said to him, "Hon, they want to move me, don't let them."

"I know Babe. I get the feeling they just want you outta here. I'll do all I can to make them keep you here."

Oddly, by now the pain wasn't nearly as intense (my appendix had already burst before the MRI and with it comes a brief feeling of relief). I was still sweating profusely and feeling delirious and Oh was I weak and sick.

A nurse came in and stone-faced announced, "Her temperature is high. We're going to keep her here during the night for observation and then we'll move her to the facility in Sun Valley first thing in the morning..."

"Please nurse, can you give her something? She's really in a lot of pain."

"I'll see what I can do..." And she walked out.

After a while, another nurse came to keep an eye on me. She was very sweet and looked in my room a few times, but she told me there wasn't much she could do unless the doctor gave her orders... So I just had to "tough it out" all that night.

Tommy took Raymond to our friend's home and then was made to stay in the waiting room for the rest of the night. While I lay there alone, I began feeling that "ebbing" sensation throughout my being. I knew that I had more than just severe flu and that my body was having a hard time keeping a hold on my spirit.

Although I knew I was ill like never before, what I didn't know was; that my appendix had now ruptured and my intestines were pumping raw feces into my body cavity and I was becoming "septic". In layman's terms, my entire abdominal area was becoming a mass of infection and it would be over 14 hours before any of the "professionals" knew or even cared about it.

When morning finally arrived, just before they were about to transfer me to another hospital, the daytime attending physician came into my room to make sure I was stable enough for transport. By now I was in deep, deep pain once again, for I wasn't given *any* pain medication. Knowing the limits of my body from the aforementioned NDE, I *knew* my life was barely hanging by a thread.

The doctor was a cheerful, handsome middle-aged man. Perhaps he was East Indian or Middle Eastern, but his bedside manner wasn't much better than the previous intern several hours earlier. He "chit-chatted" as all doctors do – not really "engaging" in any real conversation – sort of like he was just going through the pleasantries of chatting. I was scarcely coherent and really annoyed that he too was treating my condition so flippantly. He went through the motions of "checking me", asking the same stupid pregnancy questions as the night guy. After touching my distended abdomen, I nearly screamed at him to please look at my MRI film! For whatever reason, he seemed disinclined to do so, but he hesitantly opened the envelope anyway, perhaps to just appease me.

Glancing at the picture taken **several hours prior**, he suddenly GASPED very loudly "O my G*d"! A look of total horror came across his face and he yelled loudly to the nurses outside the room. As several people came dashing into the area, I couldn't understand their language, for I was feeling very peculiar and rather disconnected from the whole event, when they all hurried in and frantically made preparations to wheel me out.

Jesus Christ was the first
to bring the value of
every human soul to light.

--- Harnach
Jewish New Testament Scholar

Chapter 4

I See The Savior

That odd ebbing feeling was now increasing inside me. I heard a loud buzzing in my head that seemed to become stronger and more intense. Perhaps the buzzing distracted me or perhaps my body finally just "let go"; either way, the overwhelming pain that racked and tormented me for days was now gone! I was FREE! No... no, it was more than just the freedom from physical pain, I WAS COMPLETELY LIBERATED!! Something incredible had just happened to me. Still, it was almost imperceptible, a totally *normal* event, like somehow I've *always* known it would be. In one moment I was racked with unbearable pain and in an instant it had vanished. Like turning on a light after stumbling around in a pitch-black room – the contrast is inexpressible. I thought to myself and have reflected on it time and time again; "If this euphoric state is *dying*, why do we fear death so much?"

Had I passed into another dimension? I don't know. I cannot scientifically or mechanically explain what happened. All I know is, every one of us will go through something like this – perhaps not *exactly* as I did. For example, I never passed through "the tunnel" as so many others do. My transfer was instantaneous. Again, I don't know why. Nevertheless, once we do "pass through" to the "other side" and look back, we will have a feeling of freedom that we had actually known *forever*; even before we came to this beautiful earth. Like removing a dirty pair of glasses for clean new ones, our perception will suddenly become eternal, *if we allow it*. We might see former friends and family whom we knew forever, long before our earth life. We will be so happy to be with each other again, knowing that we have finished our work on the earth, never to have to leave each other again.

We will have the sensation of "returning home". I love the words of William Wordsworth:

Our birth is but a sleep and a forgetting:
The soul that rises with us, our life's Star,
Hath had elsewhere its setting,
And cometh from afar:
Not in entire forgetfulness,
And not in utter nakedness,
But trailing clouds of glory do we come
From God, who is our home:

Truer words have never been written.

It is an inescapable fact that each of us will have to return "home". In other words, each of us will have to die. Strangely enough, in my case, I didn't really know I had died. All I could remember was that I was no longer "present" in the hospital lying on a gurney with frantic people surrounding me. In fact, I don't really know when I left that hospital at all. I only recall that I was somehow instantly transported into this place of total peace and tranquility. And all of that horrible pain was gone.

Now I was wearing a beautiful white dress that seemed to be radiating bright light. Then, as I looked closer, I saw that the light wasn't coming from the dress at all, but rather, the material was sort of "see through" and allowed the light to radiate from my now glowing body and then to pass through it in a way that it shone with a magnificent brightness. Truly, my entire being was luminous with

49

an unearthly light that seemed to come from deep within all the cells of my body. I stood there for a while and just marveled at the incredible beauty of my hands and feet (they were naked), for they were shining from deep within, as if every cell was releasing light and energy.

As I pondered this, I began to notice that I could actually see myself as if I was standing back, in the "third person", *while at the same time* I could see and comprehend from my own normal point of view – all at once! My whole body was a dazzling display of light; it was all so beautiful! I could see my long black hair, but it too shone with an unreal bluish aura that came from within. I wished Tommy were here to see this!

While in this place of serenity, I can vividly recall that I was surrounded by bright clouds, for lack of a better term (they too were so beautiful!). Then, there was this magnificent stairway of the most exquisite white, almost like see-through marble with a golden hue. It was leading down directly in front of me. I also noticed that there were many other clouds, if again, that's the right word, as I descended down into a beautiful world of which there are no words adequate for description. Peace, joy, happiness, tranquility, serenity; all depict, yet *barely* touch the feeling, the impressions, the "texture" of this spiritual realm.

Again, what made it all the more bizarre was, I could actually "see" myself walking through and experiencing all this. It was as though I was seeing in a 4th, 5th, and 6th… dimensions. My ability to see, feel, and comprehend seemed limitless. I knew I could ask *any* question and the answer would somehow come to me immediately in crystal clear clarity. But what questions to ask? At the time, I was completely awestruck and quite dumbfounded, so I just kept moving forward and down that wondrous stairway. I knew I was being drawn towards something that was grand and marvelous, but at the time I didn't know what.

It appears that all physical laws, as we know them now, are either suspended or simply not present in the world of spirits. The basic law of gravity, for example that is so important to us on earth, somehow is superseded by another "natural" law of which I cannot explain. I say I was "walking", but really I was "floating" down the stairs and I "floated" everywhere throughout my visit(s) in the spirit world. Also, I could *see and feel* everything around me and comprehend *all* the sensations flooding into my physical and mental sensories; as if my brain was a combination of all the worlds' most powerful supercomputers hooked together – only infinitively stronger and more capable of discernment. I simply could not get over that feeling! What a rush!

As my mind began to grasp this "new" special power of comprehension, I looked down and in front of me was the landing of this stairway I was "walking" down. There I could see the figure of a man. I immediately could feel His supremacy; for I knew in an indescribable way that His essence filled all eternity. His visage radiated with a brilliant hue of white, golden, and blue light that was much brighter than my own but also seemed to penetrate every fiber of my being. His appearance was brighter than 10,000 suns, yet my eyes could easily gaze upon Him without having to squint.

I knew instantly who He was, for He radiated with a luminescence that surpassed anything of earthly origin. "Light", hardly describes His aura. Pure LOVE is close, but seems too shallow a verbal description, at least in the context(s) the word "love" is used today. Yet LOVE and LIGHT are the closest words in the English language I can come up with.

I could actually feel myself being drawn to Him like a child to a loving parent who's "been away too long". There I was, standing in front of the Savior of the World, the Christ, the Creator, the Word of Life, and the Light of the World... It was God Himself. And I knew that He is *the best friend* I have ever had throughout all eternity. I have known and loved and *worshiped* Him forever!

As I drew closer to Him, our lights merged and I could feel His supreme love wash over me from head to toe. He was smiling and I could tell He was glad to see me *again*. Although He had known me forever, I sensed He missed me while I'd been away. He knew me so well. I noticed that his arms were drawn out as if to embrace me like I was a child returned home from school. I immediately, ran up and hugged Him; as if I had done it a million times before, with all the love, affection and adoration I could muster. I was with my Lord Jesus; I was *home at last.*

He is a large, extremely majestic man and as His arms enclosed around my tiny frame; I knew that He accepted me for what I am and that He was not put-off by my desire to hug and embrace Him. Rather, I could feel His genuine love and pleasure for my childlike behavior.

Dumbfounded and completely overwhelmed, I was at an absolute loss for words, for I had not expected this encounter to take place. Well, at least not until I had *died* anyway! I blurted-out the only thing I could think of;

"YOU'RE SO AWESOME!"

It was *true* and I repeated it several times as He held me even tighter. My emotions were overpowered with a consuming, unspeakable joy; I ecstatically exclaimed the next thought that came into my mind;

"Now **I KNOW** you live, now **I KNOW** you're my Savior..."

I said that because my belief in the Lord while on the earth was, albeit strong, nothing but the dimmed "match light" of faith that we all have to share. Now however, embracing Him there in that beautiful place, *verified with a surety* that He is my **Savior**, and my **Lord**, and my **King**, the **Living Christ**, my **God.** He is **MY JESUS** and now I *knew* that He lives!

All presumptions of guilt or sin no longer mattered; as I was now in complete harmony with this magnificent Being of perfect form and character. I felt a rush of elation that words cannot describe when my spirit drank deeply of the *living waters* that flowed from my Lord. Now I knew that I would no longer have *any* doubt or concern about my place in the universe or my relationship with Him. The feeling of peace I basked in was so exquisite and intense, that I instantly understood that *this* is where I belong. On earth I was a stranger, a traveler, a foreigner, and a vagabond; now I was home again in the arms of the pure love of Christ and *nothing else mattered*. I wanted to stay forever.

I reluctantly broke the embrace and I put a slight space between His body and mine. He gently held me by my shoulders and I looked up into those intense, yet loving eyes; when He looked into mine, He saw tears of unspeakable joy and bliss. His thoughts became audible in my mind and sunk deeply into my heart when I distinctly heard him say:

HOME AGAIN!

IMELDA   LORAYNA   FOWLER

"Everything is going to be alright..."

These words of a surety were like a trigger that all at once sent me back into my lifeless body…

Like a vacuum sucking my spirit back to earth, I instantly heard the staff of the hospital frantically expressing their concern as they were trying to revive what was left of me. I could tell they were in a desperate attempt to bring life back into my body. Now I could hear them yelling to me in loud, frantic tones, "Come back Imelda! Wake up…come back…" all the while they were performing CPR on my already sore rib cage. With a deep gasp of air, my body *jumped* back to life as if I had been electrocuted. At that instant, the pain suddenly overwhelmed me as my physical senses instantly exploded into a frenzy of agony and torment. Although still very foggy, I struggled to open my eyes as I heard them keep reiterating "…stay with us Imelda… stay with us… don't go back…!"

I wanted so bad to go back home, to embrace my forever Best Friend; but I somehow sensed that wasn't what *He* wanted. So in humble obedience, I accepted the pain of returning to my tormented body with the reassurance of my meeting Jesus once again, "next time". I *knew* that indeed "everything would be alright", for the God of the entire universe had just assured me it would be. It was those words of comfort, spoken only a few moments before, that gave me the strength to endure the incredible trials that were about to beset me.

Once the frenzied staff "stabilized" me, one of the nurses looked me in the eyes and said in a stern but relieved voice, "Imelda, you've been a bad girl…"

Our doubts are traitors,
And make us lose the good we might win,
By fearing to attempt.

--- Shakespeare "Measure for Measure"

Chapter 5

My Brief Return...But Only For A Moment

As I lay there in surging waves of pain, my mind, could distinctly recall the details of my visit with the Lord. Yet, despite my overwhelming suffering, the thought of Him so close, had a healing effect that is still with me to this day. I could feel the warmth of His countenance and the power of His eternal love that is completely indescribable. It was then; that the reality of where I was began to hit me.

Tubes, sensors, and needles were inserted in as many assorted angles as humanly possible into my arms and stomach. A very uncomfortable tube was crammed down my nose (!) – for what I had no clue. A weighty oxygen mask was resting over half of my face. To my left was one of those gangling steel trees (I later affectionately called it my "Christmas Tree") decorated with several types of clear liquid plastic containers. From those bottles of who knows what, came see-through tubes that dripped their way into all those painful needles and shunts, which were increasingly itching with every passing second. For some reason I had a bracelet *around my ankle,* like you'd see on a body in a morgue. The incredible discomfort I was experiencing was only balanced by my ability to reflect upon my visit with Deity. Often I found myself slipping between what we refer to as *reality* here in mortality and the *real world* of the spiritual realm.

I have to laugh at skeptics and "experts" who ridicule those of us who have had the privilege to visit the other side. What is considered "reality" on this side, is "smoke and mirrors" when compared to the fullness of life that awaits us in our eternal home. My heart pities the nay-Sayers for their blindness; as they ignorantly and sometimes arrogantly keep trying to "prove" that this life is all there is. Why they feel the need to do so is perplexing to me. Sadly, when they return home (and they will), that "reality" will hit them in the face like an iron fist.

If *you* are one of those skeptics and when in the future, you finally come to the realization that you have died (many wander aimlessly in that realm not knowing or else they are not *willing to admit* that they're "dead"); I beg of you, please, when you come to that realization, swallow your pride and JUST LOOK UP. There you will see a being(s) of light who has been hovering over you and is waiting patiently for you; he/she will guide you through the process of returning back home.

I don't know how much time had passed since coming back, but I now noticed that I was no longer in the emergency room. They had transported me from the ICU into a private room around 3:30 PM that same Friday. Near 4 o'clock, Tommy and Raymond came into my room. It was so good to see them, although they were obviously stressed-out by my situation. I could visibly see the toll it had taken, especially on my husband. We've always drawn upon each other's strengths during times of stress, but this was something totally different – a new experience altogether.

Then a terrible thing happened. With Tommy there, it was the first time I felt inclined to have a full conversation with someone; when suddenly that nasty tube going through my nose and down my throat started choking me. This was more than just uncomfortable, I was gagging and coughing-up blood and loosing what little breath I had left in me. Tommy pressed the emergency button... nothing. Again... Same response. He ran down the hallway to the nurse's station and as he put it, he "calmly" told them

HOME & BACK AGAIN

I was choking on the tube running down my throat. The nurse was probably a little jaded by hearing so many requests by over-reacting spouses three or four times a day. Nevertheless, she jumped up and made haste to my bedside. There I was gagging, coughing up blood and Tommy said I started turning a pale shade of blue, unable to breathe or move because I was so full of needles. The nurse didn't hesitate for one moment and ripped the drainage tube out of my nose. Tommy said it looked like a magician's magic trick, because that sucker just kept on pulling out – like an ugly, slimy serpent about *three feet long!*

Once that crisis was over, we thanked the nurse and she seemed surprised that both of us were so calm after that alarming skirmish. We've had so many things put on us that week, so many "crises", that this one did indeed seem like a small incident. After making sure I was comfortable and that I was no longer coughing-up blood (that nasty tube tore my throat to shreds!), she left the three of us.

Since we have never had a T.V. (we "killed" ours soon after we were married), our young son missed most of the "choking drama" while he sat enthralled by "Tom & Jerry" (a new experience for him!). Just as well, it would probably be best if he just didn't see most of this stuff anyway.

After the good nurse had finished and we were left to ourselves, I whispered to Tommy (my voice was gone), "Babe, I saw the Savior..."

"Really? Please Hon, tell me everything!"

I knew if there was anyone who'd listen and believe me, it was my loving Tommy. While I told him about my incredible encounter with Divinity, he just sat there and listened intently while gently holding my hand. Just a few years previous, he too had a brief visit "beyond", so he knew first hand of the elation and peace that awaits us when we are back home among departed loved ones. He paused for a long while – "Daffy Duck" was playing in the background – he looked at me with tears in his eyes (he has deep blue eyes with long, almost unnatural eye lashes) and finally spoke.

"Meds, if you are called home or if you feel the Lord needs

you there... I will let you go."

It was all I could do to fight back the overwhelming emotion as the love of my life was willing to surrender his will over to that of the Lord's – if that's what God wanted. We openly wept together. I tried to hug him and my son as best I could, but my body was being used in what looked like an experimental human pincushion. We talked for another ten minutes or so when another nurse came in. Tommy thought it would be best to leave now and he took the Sand-crab (Raymond) with him to get some dinner.

I had not seen this nurse before and I could tell she was on a special assignment for the hospital. Perhaps because the staff knew I had "checked-out" that morning and my condition was such that I wouldn't even last the night? She asked me a series of questions pertaining to my personal life including what religion I was, do I believe in God or do I need a Chaplain?

For some reason, I felt compelled to tell her about my near death experience, my visit with the Master, the beautiful place I had seen and the peace that awaits us all. Other than Tommy, this was the first time I told anyone about it. Her reaction was opposite of his. She looked at me in a sort of awkward way. When I later asked her and found out she was a member of the Jehovah's Witness faith, I better understood her reaction. They don't believe in *any* sort of an after-life and so I knew my words were falling on deaf ears. Although she was kind, she was deaf nonetheless. When she was finished, she left and soon after a Chaplain was sent in.

Again, I felt compelled to tell him the same thing about my "close encounter" and I could tell that he was even *more* uncomfortable with the subject of seeing the Savior. "How strange" thought I, "that a man, a *doctor* of theology, who professes to know Jesus; would be *so* uneasy with my actually meeting Him, face to face." He left me in a hasty retreat and I never saw him again.

The "Veil" Is Thin

Before I recount this next series of unusual incidences in that hospital room, I need to tell you about the "veil" or as some refer, the "film" between this life and eternity. These terms are widely used by those who have had a NDE and both are an accurate description. The "veil" is simply a thin "film" of forgetfulness or amnesia, if you will, that blocks our ability, while we live in our earthly bodies, to see or move back into the world of the spirits.

Although I don't understand the "mechanics" of the veil or how it works, you might wonder why such a mechanism is necessary in this mortal probation in the first place. It really is quite simple. If you and I could remember our former lives before this earth life and if we knew of the joyful state that awaits us, we would be completely miserable while on earth. For everything in and on earth, is but a shadow or vapor of what it is spiritually. Actually, for those of us who have seen the other side; we can easily fall into a state of depression (and many do) because *we are able* to contrast the eternal state of *complete* joy and happiness with our current state of occasional joy and seemingly constant frustration. We are here in mortality to learn what is bitter that we may know how to better appreciate the sweet. This contrast is of eternal significance.

In the world of spirits we knew little of faith and patience – yet, both are Godly attributes. There, we had little faith because we lived, walked and talked with God on a "daily" basis – remember faith is believing *without* seeing.

Patience, because in the spirit, we live in a state of what might be called "instant" gratification – as I found out later. In order for our spirits to progress, we needed to develop these Godly characteristics of faith and patience; as well as others while in this mortal "testing ground". The veil is vital to our development of these attributes.

Another point I learned is that *space* and *time* mean little to those in the spirit world. Neither present any form of a barrier or frustration like they do here. As you will soon see, a spirit body is completely unfettered by "distance"; for travel is as instant as thought. Also, in that realm, time as we know it now, simply does not exist. Knowledge also seems to be instantaneous – we just need to *ask the right questions* and asking *proper* questions, can only come through living God's laws.

IMELDA   LORAYNA   FOWLER

Why Do "Bad" Things Happen To "Good" People?

Uninformed, but usually well-intentioned people are always asking why does God "let" bad things happen, if He loves us so much? The answer is in Freedom or Agency. While in my visits to the other side, I learned that of *all* things, we eternal beings have *always been free to choose* right or wrong. In fact, in the world of spirits, we are free to *do whatever we want*! By earthly standards, you might even say we are spoiled children. However, and this is really important, *we must face the consequences of those choices* (good or bad). It is in the bad choices (whether our own, or by someone else) that bad things happen to good people in this earth life.

For example, exercising control or dominion over someone else, in *any* form of unrighteousness, is a terrible sin. Bosses, politicians or any other persons in leadership positions must be very careful to not overstep their bounds of authority. If you remember, there was only one person we know of, whom Jesus had any animosity towards (other than the Scribes, Pharisees, hypocrites and lawyers in general – all of them had some form of authority) and that was King Herod. On one occasion The Master called him "...that old fox..." and then when He was on trial, our Lord *wouldn't even look at or speak* to the wicked King – he was that despicable in the Lord's eyes! Positions of authority carry with them weighty responsibility and should be carried-out in nobility and not through force or unrighteousness.

I learned that acts of unkindness, even in the least degree, must be *accounted* for – meaning that we will have to answer for our enactments of unrighteous compulsion and coercion. But because we are "free-agents" in every sense of the word, Father in Heaven *will not* step-in to stop these unrighteous encroachments on another's rights. However, if we are the perpetrators of such evils, we *will* pay the price "to the very farthing" (about a ½ penny) – meaning, that we (they) are not going to "get away with it". His judgments are always just and perfect.

Selfishness and pride are two of the most fundamentally satanic of all sins. It is these two sins that Satan uses more than any other in his vast arsenal of diabolical weaponry. Lust for anything (money, power, houses, cars, furniture, deviant sexual desire, the list is endless...), has its *roots* in these sins and can usually account for so much pain and suffering on this earth. Again, Father will not step in, in order *for the wicked to be judged justly.*

As mentioned before, when each of us dies, we will have to render an accounting of *every second* we've spent on earth. We will see in unflinching detail, a "life's review" of every act, every decision (good and bad), every triumph or defeat; in short, *everything* ever done while in the flesh. Not only will we "see" them, but we will *feel* every emotion we caused to be inflicted upon every being (including animals) with whom we have had influence over or contact with.

Our actions, our words, our thoughts and desires; produce a wave-like energy effect that "ripples" throughout the world. Certainly this is where the concept of Karma or "the law of the harvest" has come from. If we sow good, we will reap good. Bad deeds returns bad upon ourselves. An act or acts of kindness can have a *lasting* ripple effect that fortunately, we will *also be held accountable for!* Like a pebble thrown in a small pond (this earth is indeed a small pond), its energy will affect every molecule of water within; so it is with the deeds we sow in this life.

Obviously, we must make every effort to sow good seeds! If we fail (and we all do), we must repent – simply put – we must make it right. If we've hurt someone, repair as best we can, the hurt we caused. If someone has hurt us (no matter how badly), we MUST forgive him or her or **we** will carry the burden of the *greater* sin. (You may want to read that last sentence again!) I know it sounds harsh and perhaps it seems unfair, but it is true nonetheless. *Forgiveness* and *love* are one and the same. We cannot say we "love" and yet not be forgiving.

It is only through the supreme gift of love that all the pain and suffering and all the wrong doing to our fellow man (wars and other conflicts) will cease. *There is no other way.*

Ultimately, the Lord *will* step in even as He has in times past; when the world is so ripe in wickedness, that love is completely quenched by fiery evil (as in the days of Noah and too-many other times in our world's bloody history). I hope I am not on the earth when that day takes place. Until then, the Lord expects *us* to change the world through our *individual* acts of loving-kindness. That is the very reason we have been put on this earth. Remember, we're living in a small pond...

Consider the above statements while I tell you more of my personal journey as the veil grew thinner and thinner.

I Could Go Back If I Wanted

After having dropped-off the Sand-Crab, Tommy came back the next morning. During our conversation, he saw me staring forward "out into space" for no apparent reason. We had again just discussed my "going back and staying"; if that's what I felt I needed to do. After a long pause, he asked "What is it, Meds? What do you see?"

I knew the look on my face must have been somewhat startling to him. Tommy said my countenance was glowing in a manner he had never seen before. My spiritual being could comprehend completely and naturally what I was seeing. But the physical tongue is just so clumsy and inept. It took me a moment to put into words what I was seeing. Here is my best, albeit feeble effort.

As I looked towards the confines of my small cubicle, the wall in front of me simply opened up (that's the only way I can describe it). While I looked out beyond the limits of the physical walls, I saw, *felt* and heard a group of people asking me if I wanted to go "back" with them. I knew what that meant – they were here to escort me back home. Somehow I knew it was their "job" to make my acclimation easier back into their world. As if to "sweeten" their request, the surroundings they stood in were exquisite as were they themselves. I longed to be with them and out of my aching flesh.

These marvelous beings were to be my "spirit-guides". I recognized many of them as former family members who had "passed-away". Some I didn't know from my earth life, but somehow I had *known* them forever. They seemed so excited to take me with them, for I could tell they missed me. A couple of them were even a little forceful (but not overbearing).

My answer was easy. I didn't hesitate, as I knew that my husband, our young son and our now married daughter and her young family, needed me to fulfill my calling and assignment here on earth. I also understood that, although it was *my* choice, if I left this life now, I would be cutting short my time here and that I had vital work to still accomplish. I told these, my loving family and friends that it was not my time yet and that I wanted to stay and take care of my family. With that, the marvelous vision then closed.

This experience has lead me to understand that *each of us* has a mission or missions to accomplish here on this earth. No matter how hard or difficult our lives may be, suicide is *never* an option. Each moment (even the bad ones) spent on earth will help us exponentially when we go to the other side. At that time, I could have chosen to leave, but I instinctively knew my time was not yet finished.

You might ask then, why were these good spirits trying to convince me to leave? It's really simple. They missed me. Like when a family member must travel away for school or some other important reason; we want them to stay and even though we know that it would be detrimental to their progression, it's hard to let them go. Still, we love them so much, they need to know that it's all right even if they don't leave; we will still love them. So it was with these loving spirits. They just wanted me to know that "they'd be okay" if I went with them. I look forward to our happy reunion in the near future.

Although I was still in pain and extremely uncomfortable, I had a feeling of peace and harmony left over from that experience that was indescribable.

A Terrible Vision Of The Future

Tommy would patiently listen to my endless talking about going back and seeing this... or hearing that... or looking at... While he was still in the room the wall "opened-up" again and I saw a large number of people – they looked like war-torn refugees, walking in loosely organized families or small groups. They looked as if they were fleeing some incredible disaster that either had just occurred or was in the process of occurring. They were ragged and some had no shoes. My heart went out to them, for I could feel their fear, confusion and agony.   It seemed as if all their worldly possessions were tied-up in those pitiful looking bundles I saw on their backs. They looked tired, hungry and discouraged. I could tell they had been walking for days if not weeks. Perhaps they hadn't eaten for days. I cried openly for their children who clung to their parents or older siblings while they held a torn, dirty doll, or some other valued trinket or toy.

In front of this heartbreaking group were men in military-type uniforms carrying rifles and other weapons. I got the impression that they were "protecting" the group of civilians that were struggling "up the rear". I also got the feeling that there must have been another group who had gone before them and that this group was following their path. I could see that they were walking in a desert place with little or no vegetation. The ground looked parched and cracked. The sun was out and it looked to be an otherwise pleasant day. I was given no context as to the time of when this event occurred, but I did get the impression that they were driven from their homes and towns and they were trying to reach a "safe zone".

I later learned of others who had NDE's and saw similar scenes. We are all in agreement that this is linked to some future event or events here on earth. Although I was never to fully understand their significance, I continue to ponder as to why I was given this depressing vision.

Thankfully that vision closed and another came into my view, but it was even more shocking and completely depressing.

The Plain Of Hell

My spiritual eyes were suddenly opened to this enormous space of black mists and darkness. I got the idea that very little light penetrated this place; as there was what looked like a thick dark fog that blocked out nearly all the light. I knew that this region was not of this mortal sphere. As I peered through the darkness, I could see thousands, if not hundreds of thousands, disembodied spirits, mostly men and a few women, angry and dark; as their countenances radiated no light or happiness – thankfully there were no children there.

These unhappy, angry, frustrated spirits were literally grinding their jaws in the most hideous and unnatural manner. I could hear demonic howling, frightful screams and groans of terrible anguish that filled the space wherein they dwell. I could tell by their despicable actions and vulgar words that their minds were filled with hatred, violence and rampant lustful desires one towards another. Some were actually gnashing their teeth upon each other; as they were completely consumed with their own self-loathing and uncontrolled lusts. Many shrieked arrogant superiority rants and raves that led to the most violent of confrontations. They were trying to tear each other to pieces! However, their acts of violence could cause no physical damage to another spirit being; so their punches and kicks and bites had the same effect as you and I kicking thin air. Of course their frustration grew all the more when they saw no physical damage could be done, hence the air was rife with endless insults and cries of vexation. I could tell that these pathetic spirits were extremely self-centered and narcissistic. My mind thought, "we 'reap what we sow' during our mortal probation".

This terrible "plain of the damned" seemed to be more of a *state of being* than just a location. From my vantage point, I can only describe it as being a wickedly "hot" place. Not heat like that of the sun or of fire, but more like a seething burning of despair and loathing. This perfectly created an atmosphere cankered with a constant and seemingly hopeless eternal damnation, where "their 'worm' never dies". This, in turn, created its own latent air of mass regret and anger, which permeated this wretched place of hell.

To look upon this seemingly endless plain, felt like I was looking into some sort of prison wherein escape would appear impossible. It was when I thought upon this, I realized that all these miserable beings had to do is "look up" and they would be healed. Their "escape" from hell *was* possible by a simple, humble act of submission. In the act of "looking up", they would have seen the angelic loving beings hovering over them (perhaps family members?), waiting, hoping to *release them* from their "eternal damnation". Until then, they lovingly waited – unnoticed above them all.

During this most depressing, terrible vision, I also understood that these miserable souls were not there because of some sort of cosmic *punishment*; rather, they were being *rewarded* for their decadent, selfish deeds lived during their mortal probation. I was also strongly impressed that these pathetic spirits had wasted their earthly lives on the pleasures of the body, while not developing their spiritual side. They didn't develop their goodness, because they "put-off" the Light of Christ (that *all* men and women are given when they come into this world). Because they snuffed-out that light, "spiritual things" no longer had any value to them and they *entirely wasted their days of mortality!* I recognized many of them to be of the wealthy class of earth beings (**not to say** that they were all once "rich" or that all wealthy people are going to hell, hardly!). Because of the "power" they held on earth, they became a "law unto themselves", having put off the laws of God for their own lusts and desires. It is a universal natural law that "misery seeks company". I knew that this place of miserable beings is where spirits wind-up or perhaps even *seek after,* if they reject the basic laws of God (His commandments) and purposely rebel against their innate spiritual natures.

I have never experienced a more wretched place or feeling. My spirit drew back. I wanted to leave. Fortunately I did.

My Visit Into The Garden

All these open visions occurred while Tommy sat at my bedside in the hospital. He later told me that during these visions, he could see my facial expressions and my very countenance would change according to what I was witnessing. He would occasionally ask me, "what do you see now..." or "tell me more..."

Immediately following my visit to the plain of the damned, I was allowed to leave (gratefully) and visit a place that totally contrasted to that previous awful scene; for I was suddenly and instantaneously transported to the most exquisite garden. It was unlike anything on earth. It was perfectly organized in a manner that could have only been determined by heaven. My ears could detect the most pleasant sound of harmonic chimes or blissful tinkling from an unseen heavenly instrument. I saw the most colorful plants and trees and flowers arrayed in vivid hues that are beyond description and that no painter's pallet on earth could duplicate. Each flower, tree and shrub radiated their own celestial energy and light. Each was in harmony with the sounds, sights and smells; it was all a perfectly orchestrated symphony.

I've always been drawn to the natural beauty of plants, particularly flowers. When I saw these heavenly masterpieces, my heart leaped for joy. I walked up to the most dazzling bouquet of vivid color I have ever witnessed. As I went to smell them (a passion of mine), I could *see, feel and hear* their joy; that I, one of the *higher order of beings* would actually take notice of them. It was almost as if they were *performing* for me. I know it sounds funny, but I *could feel their excitement* as they "did their best" to put on a dazzling display of light, heavenly scented perfumes, and sound.

Afterwards, I thanked them for their performance (odd, I know, but I've always talked to flowers and shrubs and I do so even more now that I know it is so appreciated) and I told them, I was quite impressed by their display. A feeling of joy and happiness flowed out from them and filled my heart with unspeakable pleasure, knowing that I had taken of my time to "visit" with them.

I could plainly see other women enjoying the grounds of this special place of beauty and peace. They conversed in low, reverent tones as they joyfully tended to their duties or simply "took in" the beauty that surrounded them – as I was doing. They were arrayed in perfect white dresses that went down to their ankles and covered their arms to their wrists – the same raiment I wore. Their own countenance's glowed with a light that came from within. I knew, like me, they too had been purified by the light of Christ, as sin and remorse were replaced by virtue and purity.

I could see and hear a marvelous cascading waterfall and stream that lead into a sparkling lake and that *the very water itself* had its own intelligence and life. It seems incredulous, but I could feel the *water's* joy – for even it knew, as did the flowers, the glory they were giving to God because they were "choosing" to live in the prefect order that I found them. I sensed their collective happiness as they were "doing their best" to fulfill their measure of creation. The water's flowing filled the air with this constant soft reverberation that seemed to echo the music of eternity.

My heart soared and I longed to bring my family there and remain forever! I kept asking Tommy, "Oh, don't you see it? It's all so beautiful! Can you smell it, Babe?" It was peaceful beyond description and I look forward to when we would all be there together someday.

When this vision ended, my heart was filled with thanks and gratitude. Tommy and I discussed it and the other glimpses in detail. He was moved as we shared our feelings with one another. Together we tried to put meaning on those seemingly random events and visions.

Later that evening Tommy left to get Raymond and I had another visitor from San Pedro. We talked until 8 o'clock that night which is closing time for anyone not part of hospital staff or related to patients. When she left me, I was alone in my room where I tried to "get a handle" on what had just taken place during the past couple of days.

The Power Of Thoughts – An Out Of Body Experience

As I lay there quietly contemplating my predicament and pondering what I had learned, I could feel a deep sense longing for my husband and son. I wanted more than anything else to be with them at that moment.

Instantly, I found myself catapulted to where I was standing outside our boat and I passed-through the hull and then into the salon (living room). This had been our home for the last three years. I could plainly see my husband and our little boy in the small cabin bed, forward of where I stood. He and little Ray were lying in bed together playing with our little black min-pin dog, Diva. I was a little annoyed that she was on our bed, but that soon passed, as I just felt so happy to be at home again! I smiled and breathed a deep sigh of relief.

Suddenly I realized that they hadn't noticed me come in. Even Diva was oblivious to my presence, for she always barks her loud, often annoying salutation when she greets me. "How odd..." I thought.

I tried to get their attention, but they couldn't hear me. Why were they ignoring me? I got right in Tommy's face:

"Hey, guys, it's me...I'm right here..."

No response. Not even a growl from the dog. How could this be...?

I then thought of our daughter who happened to be visiting her Aunt Debbie, in Idaho. Alona had taken their new baby there to show-off over the holiday. How I wished I could see them. Instantly, I was standing by their bedside watching them sleep peacefully. I tried to shake them awake, but my hand didn't seem to have any substance and therefore it just passed right through her shoulder. Frustrated by my inability to communicate with my loved ones in the U.S., I then thought of my family in the Philippines.

Once again, I was inexplicably conveyed there faster than the speed of light and now I saw my mother in the wonderful little home of my childhood. She was busy hand-washing clothes out by our old hand pump. This was a place I knew so well as a child and teenager growing up, because I had also washed the family laundry countless times there. I hadn't seen my Mama for a few years, since my Papa passed-away. She looked the same, only a little older. Oh! It felt so good to be home! Once again, I tried to get her attention, but with the same results.

However, by this time I was finally beginning to understand that the "substance" part of me was still lying, battered and bruised, in a hospital bed in San Pedro. Now that I better understood how things work and what was actually taking place, my frustrations left me. I smiled at Mama, telling her that I love her.

Suddenly, I felt an urgent need to return to my body. I had been away too long! At an instant I was back in my tormented, tortured, house of clay, gasping for breath while the monitors next to me were beeping loudly.

The overwhelming sensation of returning shocked me into a level of pain that cannot be described as doing something as simple as breathing became excruciating. I had forgotten that the nurses in intensive care had hooked up monitors so they immediately knew that my heart and breathing had stopped. They frantically rushed in to check on me. By that time I had regained control of my breathing; my heart rate started returning back to normal. They became angry with me; because they thought I was taking off the little diodes causing the monitors to "flat-line". But when they checked and found them all still hooked-up, they were at a loss of what had actually happened.

Dying **Can** Be A Frustrating Experience

My "out of body" experiences are in no way unique. As mentioned before, when a person "dies" the event is as natural as taking your next breath. The "mechanics" of death (war, violent car crash, heart attack, etc.) can seem traumatic on this side of the veil, but to the individual who experiences it, they do not feel *any* pain when leaving his/her body (death). It is when we are "allowed" to linger in that body after the trauma; that's when it can get really unpleasant.

Because the event is so natural and "seamless", some who pass to the other side don't even know they are dead (like myself in the beginning and at subsequent times). That may seem like some kind of oxymoron, but it does happen. Here are just a few examples of how this can be:

There are times when a person may *erroneously* feel their work on earth is not yet finished or they may be *completely obsessed* with a business project or with their worldly possessions or relationships (an over-doting mother). Even though the evidence is overwhelming that they died (they can see their lifeless body lying on a gurney with a sheet over themselves or they may be slumped-over after a car crash…), sometimes these individuals can't accept that actuality. Although frustrated (as I was), they will spend too long making an effort to intervene with their former family and associates trying to complete that task(s) or hoard over their "hard earned" possessions. Of course, as we've seen, they can do nothing but watch in annoyance, while those on this side try to "get back to their lives"; completely oblivious to the vexation they are causing their deceased family member/friend.

Others might be too prideful to admit, "they were wrong" about the afterlife. Again, even though the evidence is overpowering, their pride will keep them from progressing forward. Hence, they may aimlessly wonder this earth, to and fro seeking in vain a rationalization of their new state of being.

Still another soul might have committed serious sins (acts against God's universal laws or commandments – like murder). These people usually fear death more than anything else. Their spirits tell them they will have to face the consequences of their misdeeds. They know in their "hearts", they will be held accountable for their acts performed in this life. They **know** what their *reward* will be.

I am of the opinion that it is these obsessed and often disobedient spirits who wander this earth and "haunt" former places where they feel most comfortable. Upon their death, many return to the "scene of the crime" where they may have performed their acts against nature (all *sins* are simply breaking some sort of natural law(s)). All are unhappy. All are frustrated.

Once again, the solution is uncomplicated. All they need to do is swallow their pride (it is pride that got them there in the first place) and look up to The Light above them. Repentance is an *eternal* principle – the Lord's Grace is sufficient on *both sides* of the veil. Does that mean we can put-off repenting and continue in our sins while we live in this life – after-all, can't I just repent when I get there?

I'll let you answer that question.

Life is too short to be little.
There are too many worthwhile causes to serve –
grumbling over past painful experiences,
brooding over injuries, conjuring up ways to get even,
smarting over grievances until we cannot sleep.
Life is too short!

--- Benjamin Disraeli

Chapter 6

The Pain Of Recovery

That night and the next few days, consisted of me slipping in and out of my body and I was finding it hard to sleep; for the second I would close my eyes to relax, I would discover myself outside my earthly shell – a totally natural sensation. Perhaps part of the reason I had so many "out of body" experiences, was my spirit wanted to get away from all that pain? Whether for that reason or not, the veil was virtually non-existent for me at that time. It was as simple as taking off a dirty, worn-out coat and hanging it on a rack. It had become that easy for me to just "check-out".

One of my problems with this new found mode of "transport" ("...beam me up Scottie...") was every time I would leave, my vital sign monitors would go ballistic, sending the poor night shift nurse running into my room. However, there still must have been some kind of "connect" for me, because about the time she'd arrive, I'd be back in my body and my breathing and heartbeat, albeit rapid sometimes, would come back to "normal". Although completely unintentional, it was a terrible way to "tease" a compassionate health care provider.

IMELDA   LORAYNA   FOWLER

One example that illustrates how precarious I was "hanging-on" is exemplified by my constant high temperature. I was given large doses of antibiotics; for my body was still fighting off the "septic" infection for more than 14 hours.

A graphic, if not morbid way, to illustrate this would be like someone cutting a large hole in your stomach region and then pouring a couple pounds of putrid, liquid, untreated sewage into the wound and letting it "fester" for 14 hours – now *that's* what I call *septic*! And septic I was, for days my body temperature was at critically high levels. You can only imagine the physical pain I was enduring – it's no wonder my spirit wanted out of there!

By now, my otherwise dark brown skin was pale and drawn. My weight was beginning to drop dramatically (I didn't have much to lose in the first place!). But perhaps the worst physiological damage I was experiencing – and any woman reading this will relate – was my once flat, hard stomach (my abs) was distended and swollen with the effects of infected bodily fluids. I had a gross, dripping tube shoved into the side of my belly, to suck-out the subsiding infection. "This... after all those sit-ups..." thought I. I guess I really do have a vain side of me after all?

It was sometime on Saturday that I took my first walk since the surgery. Like any active person will attest, the hardest part of convalescing is laying around. I was antsy to get moving. I remember rising up from my bed with a concerted effort, and dragging my "Christmas tree" with me, along with all those tubes and wires sticking out of my body. My first goal was to attempt the simple task of moving down the inner hall to the nurse station and back; a total distance of about 100 feet. After a while it became easier with time, but those first tries were painful and I began to wonder if I would ever be allowed to move about normally again.

Before I knew it though, I was pulling my little life support system all over the place, visiting and becoming friends with everyone on my floor. I think the nurses were surprised at my rapid recovery. I got to know everyone on a first name basis, why they were there and when they'd be leaving. Before too long the staff was having to remind me to "get some rest, Imelda". What they didn't know was, I was still leaving my body every time I tried to just close my eyes and take a nap.

Sleep deprivation was starting to take a toll on my body.

"Babe, You've Got To Get Some Sleep!"

On Sunday, Tommy and Raymond came by again, as well as several more people from my church and community in a steady stream. These well-wishers came with flowers and other thoughtful tokens of love. In fact, I recorded in my journal that 23 people visited me in that room just on Sunday alone. I remember the calls from my mother-in-law and my daughter who was visiting cousins in Idaho, along with my sister-in-law, Debbie who also lived in Idaho. It was a good day for me, as I began to feel I was on the road to being healed. For whatever reason though, I was not allowed a full night's rest during the entire time I spent in "recovery".

Much of my problem was I *knew* that there were many people in that facility who felt little in the way of hope. Some were in despair, a few were extremely lonely. There was so much sadness and pain all around me and when I was in "the spirit", I could feel their pain keenly. I just couldn't fathom leaving them in that condition while I "went to take a nap". I know it sounds odd, but I felt guilty when I left them to tend to my own "selfish" needs (like sleeping).

When the nurses helped me to lie down for some much-needed rest, the minute my eyes closed, my spirit would be right back up and "out" tending to the needs of my new friends. Even though they couldn't hear or see me, I would comfort them with peaceful words or I would kneel beside them to ask the Lord for their speedy recovery. When I would return to my body just a few minutes (seconds?) later, I would grab my "tree" and go to minister to them in the flesh. Even with all these good intentions, the physical toll of not sleeping was having a profound effect on my already wracked body. I think I better understand *now* (not then) the Saviors admonition "to not run faster than we are able to bear".

75

Yes, yes, although I was running around doing "good" to my fellow man, it was literally killing me.

By the time Monday had rolled-around, my room was filled with cards and beautiful flowers from so many friends and well-wishers.   How thankful and humbled I felt for their love and concern for me in the form of prayers! By now they had taken all the heart monitors off me (I think they were just tired of so many "false alarms"!), but I still had an I.V. and that yucky conduit poked into my side, with its own clear pipe and jar full of infectious goo. My husband and son came to visit me several times that day; Tommy to help in my recuperation, Ray-Ray to watch Looney-Tunes.

While my loving husband and I conversed, I could sense he was worried about my sleep habits or lack thereof.   One time, before he went to drop-off our son at a friend's home, he left me with explicit instructions to GET SOME SLEEP! When he returned just a few minutes later (he'd forgotten something), I wasn't in my bed. Knowing me all too well, he asked the attending staff if they saw me walk by? "Oh yeah, she's in room..."

There I was holding Mable Glick's hand, comforting her. After a moment or two, Tommy gently took my hand, politely excused us and led me back to my room. In the mean time, I was talking non-stop about Mable's condition and how I felt I might be able to help her. He could see I was fast recovering from the physical *trauma*, but if I didn't get some sleep soon, it would all be for naught.

He laid me down in bed and sat by my side. I couldn't stop talking about everything I'd done, all the places and deceased family members who I had visited and the messages they had for him and all the new things I had learned while in the spirit world. I was so excited about my new found ability to travel anywhere my mind would take me and all the new insights I'd been given while I was away... and so on and so on...

Tommy later told me that although I was speaking in complete and coherent sentences, they were running together and spilling-out as fast as my tongue could form words. Even though I am an energetic and totally animated person, I have always made it a point to never be "out of control" of my emotions or mannerisms. Simply put, I wasn't myself and he knew it.

After he put me to bed, he sat there with me and I immediately went into a fitful REM sleep. He said my eyes were dancing around like two cats were fighting under my eyelids. He watched me for several minutes. Externally, I was showing that I was (finally) totally passed-out. What he didn't know was that I had already left the room and was back at Mable's beside. He stayed with me for about another ½ hour and once he felt satisfied he had attained his objective, he left the room. Because of the ability for a disembodied spirit to see in several dimensions at once, I knew he a had left my bedside and since my spirit could *only do so much* with my new found friend (remember she couldn't see, hear or feel me), I returned to my body and *walked* back into her room along with my "tree" and some balloons and a bouquet of flowers to cheer her up.

That evening a friend came by to visit. We conversed for a while and the nurse reminded her of visiting hours. She lovingly fluffed-up my pillow and left me to myself.

I didn't feel one bit tired, but something inside, told me I needed to lie down. When I did, I was taken to a place I had never expected...

The Grand Council

Anyone who has had a NDE will tell you that our body basically duplicates what our spirit looks like. As I was led to understand, every single sub-atomic element of the body is made up of minute particles of *spiritual matter* or *intelligences*. This "refined matter" is in perfect harmony with each and every particle of our physical "shell" of clay – they are attracted to each other. When we merge our spiritual with our natural matter (come back to life) it can be painful to "enter" the body after one leaves. The spirit is literally "forcing" its way back into a lifeless shell and then having to regenerate the energy it needs to bring it back to "Life". The light emanating from our spirit is the very energy that brings life to an otherwise lifeless lump of clay. On the other hand, when the "mechanisms" of the body (vital organs, etc.) can no longer perform their functions, the spirit must vacate that flesh. The separation of the two is what we call "death." In primitive or simple terms, our bodies are literally "space suits" containing all that is necessary to keep our spirits here in this hostile environment until we have finished our mission and then we are allowed to return home.

When I left my body this time, I literally *floated* out of the room. The wall "opened up" once again and I glided through a "conduit", where I found myself standing in a beautiful plaza filled with beings of light. Like everything and everyone in this place, all the walls, the furniture, both animate and inanimate objects seemed to give off light. Each in its own harmonic vibration was joyfully singing praises to the Lord. There was that familiar feeling of warmth and peace that filled the air and penetrated my spirit. I could hear soft chimes or some other heavenly musical instrument. It was as if my own spiritual make up was somehow absorbing the "fuel" of energy that flowed through and around this magnificent place. The environment was filled with a warmth that seemed to echo the purity of life that radiated from the very presence of God.

I wondered why I had been summoned there. I knew it had something to do with all the *questions* that had welled up inside me after having visited countless places during my short visit(s) through but a *small part* of the eternal world. As I moved forward, I felt the distinct presence of others. I should note here, that when in the world of the spirits, people or objects are oftentimes blended together with the surrounding light or so it seemed to me during this visit. Once focused on any given object, though, the desired detail would emerge, becoming more pronounced in shape and depth. For example, I could now see that this grand hallway was made up of multiple columns of what looked like marble, which seemed to glow from within.

As I moved into this magnificent hall, I got the distinct feeling that many of those around me were related to me by marriage or birth. I knew they were all dear friends and I could see

78

Tommy's grandmother, Myrtle, whom I was very close to before she passed away in 1996. I got the impression that she had "pleaded our cause" previously in this very room; as to the various struggles our (her) families were having back on earth.

My Papa was there and many of his family. Along with Grandma Smith was her husband, Alton, whom I had never met in mortality, as well as my father-in-law Raymond, whom I love and miss so much. They were all there, along with countless other loving beings whose "job" it was to *watch over us* while we continued our individual journeys on earth. It was so good to see them all! It was a family reunion of the grandest magnitude. The pleasure of such reunions is inexpressible!

After greeting them all and feeling of their love and admiration for me (I embarrassingly felt like a an undeserving celebrity), there was again that perfect communication where knowledge, information, and understanding are transferred from one being to everyone at once, instantaneously. They knew of the struggles and triumphs I (we) was enduring on earth. My Papa beamed with joyful satisfaction as to the work I was *trying* to do on earth, but we seemed to be forever running into "road blocks" that kept us from progressing. They told me that I was to give a "report" of our lives thus far and I was to "plead my cause" with them before "The Council". After they had gathered around me and imparted of their love and support to me, they began to part and form a corridor in which I felt I needed to walk (float) past them towards the center of this vast assembly hall.

Conversation in the spirit world is quite unlike ours in this coarser domain. When we communicate on earth, our vocal cords move air in such a way that it produces words and sentences, which of course, are picked-up by sensors in our ears. Duh!

Communication in the spirit realm is with thoughts. Our thoughts there become *instant, perfect* communication. Whether for good or evil, they are put out there for all to "hear". I understand now why it is so important to guard our thoughts and to learn to discipline our minds. For in that place, there is no way possible you can deceive someone by "holding something back", for your deception would be broadcast the instant you thought it! It was no wonder that I was surrounded by the most pure beings in the universe. In their *individual quests towards perfection*, they had learned to purge themselves of all ungodliness. Part of that purging process is the *discipline of thought*.

Regardless, an overwhelming sentiment of hope, faith and charity filled my soul; for they were aware of our troubles and the various financial and physical struggles Tommy and I had had to endure together. It was *they who had been working with us* to help us to succeed. They knew our joys, our pains, our frustrations, and our successes and our failures.

As I continued forward, I began to sense a feeling of great nobility and awesome power. It was not only emanating from my friends and relatives, but there was something infinitively grander and more powerful than they all. In front of me were several men, behind a large banquet-like table that extended out from either side about twenty feet and formed a natural barrier between them and us. As I moved closer I noticed they too, were standing.

I could easily see their features. Some were taller than others and a few wore beautiful white beards; all were dressed in similar white robes to mine. They were in number about a dozen. Somehow I knew that these men where "in charge of things". I could also see the Lord, for He stood in the middle of this group. What made it all the more overwhelming was that God-the-Father Himself – our Heavenly Father, was also present. The combination of these powerful beings of light was awe-inspiring, as I was now standing directly in front of this Assembly of God's Chosen. It was the Grand Council of Heaven.

By this time, I was standing there by myself as the other relatives and friends were still nearby but a little in the background. I sensed that I was about to "give a report" before these men.

What happened next, I am not comfortable relating in this forum. It is much too personal and therefore I fear it will be held up to ridicule. Suffice to say, that I spoke to the Council with power and ability; a *boldness*, that I had never experienced before. Nevertheless, I spoke what was in my heart as I gave my report and pleaded my case (for lack of a better term) before the Greatest Beings in all eternity.

I stood before the Council for what seemed like a long time. While I was emotionally "speaking" before this panel of God's noblest beings, suddenly the unexpected occurred...it was something I didn't think would ever happen.

Jesus suddenly stepped down from his elevated place and stood between me and the Council of men. He towered over my four feet ten inches, as I estimated His height to be over six feet. I looked up into His face, and, while looking me in the eyes; He slowly got down on his knees and gently embraced me. At first it was a simple hug, but gradually His hold became a firm grip as I began to feel the powerful love of his countenance gently penetrate every cell of my embodiment. Indescribable peace and love flowed through me and over me. I glanced over at the Council and I could feel their love and approval as well. Then I looked at the Father and I could feel of the deepest love and adoration He had for His Son, who had done so well in doing *all* that He had *ever* asked of Him. Pride isn't the correct word, but He was beaming His love and consent for me *through* His Son (if that makes sense?). *The love The Father has for His Son is beyond anything I have ever experienced or **will ever** experience!*

I knew now that He (They) had accepted my plea, as my thoughts became His with these words, "Everything will be fine..." He then promised me that "...everything you and your family have done will be rewarded to you."

I couldn't help but react as I said those same words as before, "Thank you Lord...you are so awesome!" What else could I say?

While still on his knees, He then broke the embrace and put his hands on my shoulders as I heard Him say, "But now *you* have a choice..." then while still looking straight into my eyes, "...you can stay with me if you like, or you can go back. The choice is yours."

I knew that I wanted to stay more than anything else, but I also knew that I was needed back on earth; so I replied, "Thank you Lord... but if you don't mind, Tommy, Little-Ray and Alona still need me..." by this time, I was sobbing.

He continued to look at me with those blazing eyes like fire and then He gently kissed me above my forehead while He quietly said, **"You have chosen the better..."**

Lord, make me an instrument of Thy Peace.
Where there is hatred, let me sow love.
Where there is injury, pardon.
Where there is doubt, faith.
Where there is despair, hope.
Where there is darkness, light...

--- St. Francis of Assisi

Chapter 7

An Encounter With The Adversary

When I left the Savior and the council room, I found myself in an unusual area where I had never been before. This place had no walls and no ceilings, just a kind of empty space – almost like a "waiting area" of sorts – I sensed I was where I needed to be for that moment, but for what I did not know.

Then I found myself in the company of a stranger. He wore a dark robe and was not altogether scary or unpleasant at first. Still, *unlike* all the other spirit beings I had met up to this point, he didn't emit any light and had an appearance that made me suspicious and uncomfortable.

"I think you've made the wrong choice to return back to earth." These were the first words he "spoke" to me. He was moving around me as he "talked", almost like I was being interrogated in a cheap old detective movie. Before I could reply, he started in again.

"Think about how hard your life is there. Your husband is unemployed and you're not making enough money in real estate to live a happy life. Why would you want to go back to *that*?"

I was somewhat in shock, because at that time my real estate business was doing well and we were quite happy. Still, I knew I was not in my body, yet here was this smooth-talking spirit being,

83

trying to talk me out of what I already knew to be true. I tried to interject, but he continued his banter.

"He doesn't really love you, you know. If he did, he'd work harder to buy you a real house and not some tiny little boat to live on."

Now he was making me angry, but when I showed that kind of negative emotion, he seemed to feed off it and I could tell he was quite pleased with himself for having "ruffled my feathers".

I countered, "You don't know what you're talking about..."

He cut me off in mid sentence, "I've seen your struggles and I know the pain you've had to deal with. I really feel sorry for you. Your husband's lazy, that's why he's not working. Don't you think you would be happier if you just stayed here?"

This kind of exchange went on for some unknown length of time, as the evil spirit, this minion of darkness, was determined to talk me out of returning back to earth. Since I now knew that he fed off any negative energy I could produce, I didn't allow him the pleasure of "getting to me". While time passed, I sensed that he was becoming more and more angry as I resisted his tempting offers to abandon my torn-up body which; if I was to think about it, wasn't such a bad idea after all.

But that's how he operated, by telling half-truths and I realized that he was appealing to my baser instincts of pride, comfort, bodily appetites and worldly pleasures. His arguments were never blatant or raucous, but he always used subtle sarcasm and insidious accusation. He tried to make me feel as if *he* was "on my side".

I knew I had, just a few moments before, been told by the Savior himself, that I "...had chosen the better" and therefore I was justified in my desire to return and fulfill my mission on the earth. It was the Lord's reply to me that gave me strength against this very persuasive impish demon. I knew that there were many who needed my talents and abilities back on earth. I also felt, I somehow needed to share what I've learned from my experiences on the "other-side". In short, I knew I had a work to do and nothing this minion from hell said could persuade me otherwise. The more determined I was, the more cunning and subtle he became.

The only way to describe him is; he was made-up of pure evil and as my examination with him continued, he began to let down his pretenses of being "smooth" or "unobtrusive". If it was physically possible to radiate darkness, then this creature of the damned could do it. Seeing him now as a being of darkness, I knew that I was talking to Satan himself. I knew that this was the Adversary – the Great Accuser – in all of his wickedness, oozing with deceit, anger, lies and loathsomeness.

I perceived his thoughts as he said to me, "you know you're not a good person…why do you want to go back knowing that?"

My righteous ire was now sufficiently raised enough to respond with this retaliation, "I know you are Satan…and I have faith in my Savior, Jesus Christ…"

I could tell there was power in the very words I had just spoken. For when I used the Lord's name, Satan shrank back. Still he attacked unrelentingly, "We don't speak THAT name here… besides, your faith is weak, it's insufficient…"

I sternly replied, "In the name of Jesus Christ, I command you to depart!" With those sacred, forceful words, *this* test with Satan concluded.

The names of Deity are indeed sacred and powerful. It is no wonder he wants us to desecrate them by tempting us to profane, that which is Divine.

It was almost as if I had said some "magic words" for, at the moment the devil disappeared, I jumped back into my body. Jumped is the right word; for with that first gasp of air (like being shocked with paddles), I knocked over the tray of food and "get-well" cards sitting in front of me all over the floor. The nurse came running in upon hearing the tray and its contents hit the floor (poor girl), "Are you alright, Imelda?"

The pain of returning was a forceful reminder that the road ahead would be long and arduous. I thought about going back to the spirit world and realized that my commitment to stay in my body would bring the consequence of pain and suffering. I said a silent prayer, asking the Lord to help me become strong, so that I could overcome whatever challenges lay ahead – including any future attacks from the Forces of Darkness.

Praying during the early days of my youth in the Catholic Church and up to this point, have helped me to understand how prayer would help in anything that might confront me. It was during this time that I began to realize how I needed to face whatever the Adversary would throw at me, because I had recommitted to endure to the end. I remembered my visit with the Council and my Savior, and actually seeing God the Father. It gave me the strength I needed to support my vow to stay. By now, I was, literally, dead tired. I asked the Lord to help me to sleep, as exhaustion was now overtaking me.

Sleep did come, but it wasn't easy because the ugly terror of confronting the Adversary would occasionally seep back into my thoughts. This process would continue for some time, as the reality of what had occurred with the Forces of Darkness sometimes caused me to abruptly wake-up from my attempted efforts to get some sleep. I found that with a little prayer and earnest meditation on my vision of the Lord, peace would come and I began to relax into a feeble nap. By this time, it was Tuesday morning and the sun was beginning to rise, casting a dim light into my room.

The Importance Of Persistent Prayer And The Devil's "Due Time"

Why was I allowed to see the Devil? Or rather, why was he allowed to visit me directly, face to face, *just after* I had been with the Savior?

In order to understand the answer, we need to discuss another important topic. This is not easy for me to put into words, but I'll try. I understood that the principles of the entire universe and the way it is governed is through *universal law*. We call these laws "absolutes" or Truth. They *never change* and it is these laws that align the heavens in perfect order. But I have also learned that there is a perfect "balance" to these natural laws. When one pleads to the Lord in prayer, it is *required* that there will be an "equal time" or an opposition to that which we are praying for.

There is an old euphemism that says; "The Devil gets his due..." There's more to that simple statement than most people realize. The Devil's "equal time" was *designed for this earth life* and is to be used as a test of our character in *all* that we do, in every facet of our lives. It is part of the Divine plan of eternal progression that mankind be tested during this earth life to see if our innate nature(s) will "harmonize" with these eternal laws. The purpose of this "opposition" is to use our God given *free agency* to either do good or evil. Our choices are then weighed against these principles.

Because Satan is the great Adversary, he is *allowed* to test us to see if we will live the laws of heaven or follow the carnal laws of the devil. Earth was created for that very purpose, to allow each of us to come down here and test our character to see if we are worthy to return to the presence of God. Part of that test is to *prove* if we have enough spiritual confidence (trust in the Lord) to pray and *expect* to receive an answer. We call that process, Faith.

When we pray, our faith must be strong enough to allow the prayer to rise above the opposition according to the desire and the need of the petitioner. This law works for the "small things" we might stand in need of, as well as for the "bigger requests" we ask the Lord when praying to Him for help. This can sometimes seem agonizing and slow, but learning patience is also part of the equation of "waiting on the Lord."

During that waiting period, you will learn that Satan will get his "due time" in order to discourage and even create disheartening moods that could dilute your faith to endure. This is a principle I kept learning whenever I got closer to the Lord's Spirit. It seemed the "thinner" the veil that divided me from this world into the next, the *more* opposition I had to encounter.

I learned that these forces of darkness are actually *assigned* to create emotional or spiritual contention, which can oftentimes lead to discouragement and even depression. I also learned that *the devil cannot read your mind*, but he can read your visage or your

87

countenance, which reflect how we are feeling. Our outer countenance or aura changes its visible radiation (light) according to our moods – sort of like a spiritual "mood ring". He uses that to determine how best to oppose you. He has had thousands of years to perfect his skills, so through this process, the devil can "read" you very accurately. He will then determine what *type* of opposition to use against you.

Discouragement and depression are the strongest and most potent weapons that the minions of darkness can use against our power of faith and prayer. He uses them to foster doubt in our faith, this is in opposition to the spiritual powers of Divine Light that is given to everyone. Satan's plan is to lead us *away* from that Light. Falling into his trap is what we call "sin". Sin is simply a violation of these universal laws (or God's law) that we've been discussing. Sin literally means we are *out of harmony* with the laws that govern the universe.

I have learned the most important ways to stay away from sin is to *pray often* and *repent* or seek forgiveness when I sin. We don't have to "beat ourselves up" when we falter – for we all do and we all will. Rather, after stumbling, we just get up and *dust ourselves off*, as it were, then climb back onto whatever path we were on before we fell.

This "dusting off" process is called *repentance*. To repent simply means, we ask the Lord for forgiveness and then set out to rectify whatever or whomever we've sinned against. Then, and this is probably the hardest part, we make s*incere effort* to not recommit that sin. It's important to NEVER GIVE UP and *keep dusting ourselves off* – no matter how many times we fall. It's also important for us to *keep forgiving those who have sinned against us* – "even seventy-times seven". When we do this, we are helping our fellow spirits to better their lives on this earth through *their* repentance process.

Our prayers must be constant and determined. The idea of persistent prayer was later emphasized in a parable found in the New Testament; where the Savior told the story of a widow who *continually petitioned* an unjust judge. She badgered him to the point that he grew weary of her constant harassment to "avenge" those who had wronged her. He finally gave in to her just because, by granting her request, she wouldn't bother him any more!

The Lord said that the point of this parable is that "Men ought always to pray, and not faint." (See Luke 18:1-6)

In thwarting the Adversary's plan, persistent, *faith-filled prayer* is one of the keys to unlocking the windows of heaven.

In writing these past few pages, I grew concerned that it might seem too "preachy". But later, as I pondered many of the problems our societies face, I came to the conclusion that we have gotten away from the "basics" of righteous living. *Political correctness has become the "gospel" of our modern-day fellowship.* Surely, we must be tolerant of others and their beliefs and even their lifestyles. Still, although the Savior never condemned the sinner, He also *never condoned the sin*; rather His words were always stern – "go thy way and *sin no more*".

We must, as a society, return back to simply "being good". What does that mean? Let's not over analyze it my friends; but rather, let us live with that childlike faith we all grew up with. "Being good" simply means *doing our best* to live the Lord's commandments *everyday* and believing that when we falter (and we will!), the Lord's Grace is sufficient to heal our mistakes, both in this life and the next.

Our personal actions of faith, persistent prayer and constant repentance, will assure us that we have not only "talked the talk", but more importantly, we have "walked the walk"; no matter how hard it may be. Then, *because of His grace*, we will be brought home to live with Him forever in Paradise, never again having "to go no more out".

Lord, must I bear the whole of if, or none?
"Even as I was crucified, My son."
Will it suffice if I the thorn-crown wear?
"To take the scourge, My shoulders were made bare."
My hands, O Lord, must I be pierced in both?
"Twain give I to the hammer, nothing loth."
But surely, Lord, my feet need not be nailed?"
"Had Mine not been, then love had not prevailed."
What need I more, O Lord, to fill my part?
"Only a spear-point in thy broken heart."

--- Frederick George Scott

Chapter 8

I Finally Leave The Hospital

Prayer really can be the most powerful force in the universe. This is illustrated in both the dramatic, like Moses parting the waters of the Red Sea, or by small things like pleading with the Lord for relief of suffering or perhaps a temporal blessing that is immediately needed. Prayer can also be used as a *source of comfort*.

This happened while I was lying in my bed that morning after my encounter with the Forces of Darkness. I was in some discomfort and asked the Lord to help me endure my pain through His strength. As I did that, one of the nurses came in and turned on the television. My husband and son had come in earlier to deliver some goodies. We talked about my experience that night and when I could be released from this place.

After they left, I was watching a newsflash on the monitor mounted high in front and above my bed. On it I could plainly see there was a police helicopter circling above San Pedro near the hospital where I was presently convalescing. The news announcer was describing a grisly homicide that had occurred the previous night. I could plainly hear the police aircraft circling outside at that moment and I realized I was near a front-page story unfolding all around me! The murder scene, I later found out, was near the hospital. At that same moment, I began to feel the deep emotions of the housekeeper that was fluffing my pillow. I got the impression that she was preoccupied with what was on the news. Through an enlightened gift of discernment I knew that she was related to those involved and she was connected to the victim of this terrible incident.

I asked her if she was all right? She responded that her son was in a bad way and that he needed help. I asked her if she would like to pray with me about her son. She responded, "Oh yes, please... could we?"

I felt the Lord's Spirit strongly as I prayed for her son, who was coincidently part of the police action that was taking place. I prayed for this wonderful mother, who was beside herself emotionally. I asked the Lord to bless her and her son...

"Thank you so much", was her heartfelt reply. "I feel so much better now."

We chatted a while longer and then she had to return to her duties at the hospital.

Just after she left, a CNA (Certified Nurse Aide) came to my bedside and she was in the same emotional state as was the housekeeper. Again, through this enhanced gift of discernment, I knew she was also involved and was not happy being around the previous woman who had come in earlier. I asked if she was all right. This woman's reaction was totally different and she became very defensive when I mentioned the police investigation. I never was able to pray with her; as she said she was in "no mood to pray". Unlike the humble woman before, this seemingly prideful CNA had *forfeited her right* to seek the healing powers of God.

Prayer is like that. It is a two-way conduit that *must be initiated by us*. When we get to the other side and have our "life's review", we will see that the times we felt that God was "far away", was simply the results of *our* shutting Him out. He is and will always be waiting for us to "call Him". Opening communication with God is a good way to not only alleviate stress, but it can help even if the solution is not immediately obtainable. When we pray, we open a *direct link* to Deity, He who knows all things from beginning to end. Every person on earth has access to this power, if they would but use it.

That day, the tests that I had taken to determine the state of my health had come back positive. I was to be out of the hospital by three o'clock that afternoon. I had dressed in very loose pants and a shirt, in order not to accent my still septic, bulging tummy. My intestinal track was reorienting itself, so there was a lot of pain and discomfort in that area. I was still *barely* in the process of healing. Fortunately they finally took that gross, dripping tube out of my side, but the leftover wound was sore, both inside and out.

This was all the more tolerable because two of my best friends, Renee and Don, had flowers sent to me just as I was getting ready to leave. A co-worker named Mohammad had just given me a bag of oranges (a Sri Lankan "get well" custom). I also had an entire room full of flowers, candy, balloons and cards. When I was finally ready to go, I went around with Raymond to the other patients, many who were distraught and felt abandoned by family and friends. It took me over two hours to visit them, because Ray and I took all the flowers and balloons I had received and gave them to those who had none. I believe it brightened their day, if only for a while. It made for a good ending to what was major ordeal.

While we drove in the car, Tommy and I both noticed that I still had a relatively high fever. It would come and go, but at that moment my spirits were high, so I thought very little of it. I had now assumed that with my body healing, the veil would also return to its normal "thickness" and that my paranormal activities would cease as well. Boy was I wrong!

We drove to our church were I had the assignment as the Young Women's (youth) group leader and Tommy was leader for the Young Men's organization. Since I was their leader and despite my recent setbacks, I felt obligated to fulfill that duty – besides I love being with kids.

Around five o'clock, I arrived at the church where they greeted me with a 5-foot banner that read **Welcome Home** in big letters. Scattered around it were various individual notes of sympathy and affection that reflected their love and prayers that had been sent in my direction. This was accented by taping small candy bars to the banner that had various "sweet" messages of appreciation from the girls I love so much. I couldn't help but feel the outpouring of love from those who had been praying for my recovery.

Another Out-Of-Body

When you die, your spirit separates from your body – permanently. That's what death is – a lasting separation. Although a Near Death Experience *is* a separation, it is not permanent – hence the term, "Near" Death. As I had already experienced this phenomenon several times now, it got to the point that the "veil", which divides our world from the hereafter, became quite thin. I discovered later that many other people who had had NDE's go through similar experiences as mine.

Perhaps it was because my spirit was somehow "conditioned" to accepting the ease of which I could leave and come back now? I don't really know for sure. However, what I did know was that I was having a hard time staying in my body when I'd go to sleep. The pain of *returning* was less and less and there were times when I honestly couldn't tell if I was in my body or out. This troubling reality was graphically illustrated when I went to the park where we were having a combined youth overnighter.

There I was, still feeling very weak and sick, as my temperature was hovering around 102. Really, I should have taken Tommy's advice and stayed home; but remember, I am still a hardheaded Filipina. Besides, being around all that exuberant youthful energy was therapeutic for me. Tommy stayed close by me while I did my best to go through the motions of *looking* like I was feeling better. After all, I didn't want to bring anyone else's spirits down for my sake. Raymond was there with us, entertaining all the teenagers with his boyish antics.

Later on, I started feeling really light headed and went to sit down on one of those big picnic tables that every park seems to have. Tommy had left me for just a moment to check on "the boy" who was out playing hide-and-seek with some of the teens. It was now dark, so I wasn't noticed by anyone. As I sat there, I laid my head down to rest just for a moment.

Suddenly, I was walking around again and I wasn't tired one bit! In fact, I felt totally amazing and full of life and energy. I wanted to get involved with the kids and join in the fun that was being had all around me. I went up to another adult leader and started having a conversation with her hoping I could get more involved. We were both looking at the girls play some sort of silly game along with a few of the boys – all the time I'm talking with my friend and I'm assuming she's hearing me. After a while, I noticed she's not responding to any of my questions. Thinking she's just too absorbed with the game to talk, I wonder where Tommy and Ray-Ray are?

ZOOM! In less than a second, there I am watching them put up Raymond's little tent he got for Christmas. He was so excited! He then, started playing in it with his "Hot Wheels". I began talking to them as normally as I would have, assuming they just didn't see me coming up in the ensuing darkness. But like the conversation before, it was completely one-sided with me doing all the talking and without any response. Because I felt so good, so energetic, and so "alive", it simply never dawned upon me that I was having another out-of-body experience.

About that time I looked out beyond the park towards a trail that was surrounded by the most beautiful trees and flowers I had ever witnessed. The dark of night that was so evident just a few moments before was now gone. Everything looked to me as though I were walking at noon on a clear summer's day. How beautiful it all was! The colors were of a hue that could only be described as not-of-this-world. The brightness and shear intonations of such vivid reality were so luscious and inviting, that I couldn't help but want to walk down that meandering path. I could no longer resist those colorful flowers that were "calling" to me and I soon found myself being drawn into that forest. What was so striking about this was, I perceived and sensed that if I continued to go on, *I would not be able to return*. It frustrated me because I *really* wanted to see what was at the end of that incredible blossom lined pathway.

I was in a true dilemma, I've always been drawn to the natural beauty of flowers and trees and now I was standing before a path that directed me into a heavenly garden just like I had experienced before. I so badly wanted to see where that path leads! At the same time, an alarm was going off in my head that told me to get back into my body *before it's too late*.

Thankfully, Tommy solved my predicament with a soft nudge on my shoulder. Again, like shocking defibrillator paddles had just been put to me, my body jumped back to life with a strong gasp of air.

"Babe, are you alright?"

"Hon, what a beautiful garden path that's just sitting right there..." I pointed into the gloomy darkness in front of us. "I was about to walk down it, but I had to come back..." Thank goodness Tommy understood what was going on or he'd thought that I'd really lost it!

My head was a little light and for a moment it took some effort to reorient myself. It was then, that I finally realized that I had actually left my body again while trying to talk to everyone. No wonder they wouldn't respond! How frustrating it is for spirits who wander this earth, still connected in one way or another to it and yet not being allowed to interact! I've been there and I know how they feel. Frustrated, hardly describes the feeling.

If this book does anything, dear reader, please understand that this earth is NOT OUR HOME! We are supposed to live here for a short while, fulfill our missions (each of us has a unique mission(s) to perform) and then move-on, back home where we belong. When your time here is finished, don't be afraid. Accept what has taken place and then look for a spirit-guide; they are there waiting in the light. He/she will be there for you to make your transition back home easier.

IMELDA   LORAYNA   FOWLER

Here We Go Again!

That evening Tommy dropped me off at a friend's home in Rancho Palos Verdes, as he had to attend to his duties with the youth group. Evon is an RN who had chosen to stay at home and raise her beautiful girls while her loving husband worked and provided for them. I still had a high fever and found it difficult to sleep. I also had a hard time eating, as my intestinal track was not yet ready to accept "normal" food, so I "ate" watered-down morsels, but that only helped exacerbate my diarrhea-like symptoms.

After I settled down for what I had hoped was a long night sleep, I found it more and more uncomfortable to close my eyes. This was no doubt due to the medication and fever, but it also frightened me that I might "wander-off" again, because I was afraid next time I would not be able return to my body. Because of these variables, I was extremely tired and fatigued. Eventually, though, I did seem to drift into some kind of limbo state between sleep and death.

It was during this time, a most unusual thing began to happen. I had my little dog lying next to me and Diva would go nuts when I would "leave". Her emotions seemed to lie between aggravation and panic, for while I floated above my body, I could plainly see her nervously run back and forth. She would bark frantically, as she paced herself from one end of the small room to the other. She was clearly agitated and I wasn't sure why.

Like before, I began to feel as if I could float right out of the room. As I looked around, I realized that my pain threshold had fallen and I felt no discomfort. I certainly wasn't tired anymore. At that moment, the dog went ballistic!

Then I entered my body briefly and the pain came back as well as my drowsy state of being. I called the dog over and tried to calm her down by petting her. While I was looking down at Diva who began to relax, I started to "doze" off again...if "doze" is the right word.

As I slipped into this state, I felt light-headed (although that

96

is also an inadequate term) and I noticed my physical symptoms leave all at once. There I was, floating again; completely free and unfettered (the feeling of freedom is indescribable!). That's when Diva started going-off! Her tiny body looked like she was having some kind of fit, running back and forth at the foot of the bed. I could tell she was plainly irritated by something, but I had no idea what that might be. I started yelling at her to "shush!" but of course she couldn't hear me.

Could it be that she sensed I was leaving my body? Her barking was now almost a frantic call (no dog on earth barks louder than Diva!). The wall opened-up to another beautiful scene and I felt myself beginning to separate from the bedroom. That's when I got that same uneasy feeling that told me if I went any further, I might not be able to come back. I thought of my family and friends, when instantly I went back into my shell of "dust".

Almost immediately, Diva calmed down and her barking ceased. I began to breathe again as the pain and drowsiness came back, although the pain wasn't as severe as in previous times. As I began to relax, my friend came into the room to ask if I was okay. She said that she had heard the dog barking and became concerned. I told her what happened and we both concluded that animals have a sixth-sense about their masters and seem to know when something is wrong. I'm not sure how, but it seems obvious that animals possess their own gift of discernment.

Diva was fine now, but I didn't dare sleep that night, for fear of the "Yapper" waking everyone up in the house when I "stepped-out".

By the time Tommy got me back home the next morning, I was weary beyond belief. When I laid down with him, I went right to "sleep", but this time we kept "Bob-Barker" in the other room with Raymond!

IMELDA   LORAYNA   FOWLER

You suffer, yes. And I suffer too.
And if I see you gallantly bearing your cross,
I am reproached by my weakness, my whining,
my stubborn irreconcilability.
It is your way of meeting your grief -
that gives me heart to meet mine.

--- Charles Clayton Morrison

Chapter 9

My Recovery

Upon my arrival home, we all had a few adjustments to make. Tommy gave me some simple anti-histamine to help me stay asleep. I promised him when I left my body and I did for a few more times, I would not wander-off on some beautiful path.

Funny thing now, as my pain went from extreme to "I could deal with this", my out-of-body experiences declined. I did visit the Philippines a few more times and saw my family there. By now, I got so used to leaving my body that I knew when I got no response from loving family members or friends, that I wasn't "solid" and I needed to get back to that part of me. I remember a couple of times when we'd be "sleeping" and suddenly, I would do my *back to my body jump and gasp;* then Tommy would lean over and say, "You've been gone haven't you? Nice to have you back, Babe", as he gently patted my side.

The anti-histamine worked fine. Still, my loving husband stayed by me for several hours everyday, until I got caught up in my sleep patterns. My fever dropped immediately after I slept normally for a few days.

By now my bodyweight was down to about 79 pounds. My normal competition weight is 92-94 pounds. All that hard-earned muscle had either been burned-off by high fever or just atrophied away. Of course, it took several weeks to *fully* recover. But recover I did and I couldn't wait to get back into the gym. Thankfully, my husband/trainer knew my tendency to "over-do-it" and so he had other ideas. We started with rock-bottom training/therapy basics like just taking a short walk twice a day. My poor tummy was still swollen for a couple weeks, but it too, slowly went back to normal. Once the scars were completely healed – both inside and out – I started doing easy "crunches" to strengthen my abs and regain my "core" strength. I started out with just 10-15 reps – I was used to doing 500+ a day – so that was another humbling experience. After a while, it was on to full sit-ups for a few weeks. Once I was strong enough do some Hanging Leg Lifts and nothing "popped-loose" inside me, I knew my body was ready to start hard training once again.

Some New Spiritual Gifts Granted To Others

It is well documented that individuals who experience "deep" or persistent NDE's have special spiritual endowments given to them. I believe many of these are simply the results of having passed through the veil so many times, that it (the veil) has some "holes" in it – for lack of a better analogy. Like the act of dying itself, these gifts feel natural and don't seem too extraordinary to those who possess them. So many times, an individual will be using his/her gift(s) without realizing what they're doing.

I recall several NDEers talking about their newfound ability to predict future events. They might have been watching a state lottery on T.V., when before the number is even chosen; they'll blurt it out. You can imagine the astonishment of the others sitting in the room when he or she gets *every* lotto number right? Unfortunately, because some people are greedy beings, their first thought is to head to Vegas...

Inevitably though, that enlightened soul will realize that this gift is *sacred* and that using it inappropriately displeases God and they will refuse to squander that spiritual endowment again (usually to the great displeasure of their friends!). Whether a person was religious or spiritual before their NDE doesn't usually matter; they have been blessed with a new found sense of what is right and wrong, but perhaps more importantly, they now realize that *everything* we do on this earth... *everything* – we will be held accountable for.

I'm grateful I was not given the responsibility for the gift of clairvoyance. Indeed, those who possess this supernatural ability, often feel it is their "curse" to endure while they finish their sojourn here on this earth. Perhaps like the Midas Touch, such a "gift" could prove to be very difficult, if not nearly impossible to possess and remain happy. As I talked about before, the veil has several specific purposes, not the least of which is to keep us from becoming *too* knowledgeable. When we were children, most of us have experienced sneaking in to look at a present *before* Christmas or a birthday. We all remember too well, the major letdown we felt when it came time to "be surprised". Our lives here on earth are meant to build our character by withholding information in order for us to *first* build our *faith* and *then* our *knowledge* will become *perfect*. Like building up strength for a weight lifting competition, we start out light – an easy weight we can handle – then as time goes on and our strength increases, incrementally we add more and more weight. This is how the Lord designed faith and knowledge in this earth life to be. As we talked about before, we cannot progress without opposition.

Other NDEers have been given the ability to foresee great natural and political upheavals. They've been allowed (usually during their NDE) to see great wars that will cover the earth, accompanied by terrible natural disasters and plagues. A problem many have in sharing these experiences is; when a person leaves their body or this world, they are no longer in "time" but are now in "eternity". While in eternity, time no longer has any value and therefore, when they see these future events, the "time part" of them feels as though these things are going to happen *very soon*. The reality is that these disasters can actually be years or even decades "down the road". I remember several NDEers actually put a date or dates on future events they saw while they viewed them with eternal eyes. Of course, those dates have come and gone, but not the foreseen calamity (at least not when they *predicted* them to occur). Does this mean they are "false prophets"? I don't think so. They saw the visions, of that you can be sure. Will those disasters take place? I believe they will. However, putting a time label (date) on them can create problems for another reason.

A difficulty these gifted people face when predicting catastrophic destruction is what my husband and I call the "righteousness factor" or the "Nineveh Model". We all remember the story of the reluctant prophet Jonah. He was commanded by the Lord to preach repentance to an extremely wicked people, in the super huge city of Nineveh. If you remember, he tried to hide from his prophetic calling by escaping on a boat, but later he was thrown into the sea by his shipmates (Jonah demanded them to do it, if they wanted to survive the storm that was put upon them). A large fish (or whale) immediately swallowed the prophet and spat him up on the beach in front of Nineveh, three days later. We all remember that story, don't we?

What we forget about in this great narrative or what is not usually taught; is that he was one of the few *successful* prophets in all the scriptures! He cried repentance and told the people that if they didn't repent, *the city would be destroyed.* Then an incredible miracle took place; through his preaching, the *entire city repented* and turned to the Lord! Because of their strict repentance and subsequent obedience, the Lord spared the city – *there was no devastation or calamity.* What a wonderful story! I'm so glad we have that reference of a successful prophet and the power of his preaching.

As a little side-note, Jonah was upset that he was so successful. In fact, he was angry that the Lord didn't destroy the city! (See The Old Testament Book of Jonah and read the whole story – it's a great one!).

This "righteousness factor" or people turning from wickedness to righteousness is very powerful in altering or prolonging world events. The Lord loves all His children more than we love our own. He wants them (us) to repent because He wants them (us) to return (in righteousness) back home to Him. Remember no unclean person can return and dwell with the Father.

When trying to predict world events, a prophet's timing can be thrown-off (as was Jonah's). Even if the people turn *slightly* towards the Lord, often they will be spared the terrible tempests of destruction. However, and sadly so, the scriptures are replete with cultures and civilizations who didn't repent, and were consequently destroyed – either by natural disasters or by invading marauders (war). From an NDEer's perspective, it's the *timing* that can be and is usually wrong.

I believe I was allowed to see a future catastrophic consequence to a terrible war (see Chapter 4 of this book). Tommy and I have discussed it many times. I've pondered over it, time and time again. The only conclusions we can come to is; the Lord is warning us (me?) to be wary of government (political) alliances – for it is usually because of them that wars are perpetrated. I have no faith in the United Nations or any entity – political/government or individual that throws-out the principles of the Constitution of the United States (free agency), for a more "modern" or "progressive" standard. This book is not intended to be a political commentary, but I believe the Lord is warning us through simple people like me, to be suspicious and worried of the direction our "leaders" are taking this nation (United States) and ultimately the world.

My New Spiritual Gifts

I have been so blessed since my "death" to have the ability to see and oft times converse (though, not always) with those on the other side of the veil. Usually family members will come to me for comfort or warnings – sometimes in dreams or open "daylight visions". Occasionally, they will just want to "hang-out" with me. I know, I know, hangout seems a little too casual sounding. Nevertheless, it is true. There are countless times when I will close my eyes and be transported (not the right word) to where we are standing face to face, looking at each other for no apparent reason, other than just to say "hi" or "I'm here with you now". Interestingly, unless I am out-of-my-body, we cannot verbally communicate with each other – their vocal cords cannot "push air" and it seems while I'm still in my body, the powers of psychic communication or telepathy (again, an incorrect description of what is actually happening), are not present – the veil just seems too thick.

I don't like the terms psychic communication or telepathy for spirit-to-spirit communication. These words are too vague and incomplete. For when one righteous spirit communicates with another, that 4th, 5th, and 6th... dimension thing, "kicks-in". The connection is not only instantaneous, but also absolutely perfect in every aspect. You can hear, see, feel, smell, etc. what is being conveyed – which is tough to write about when using clumsy words.

Although I am not a bold or an unrestrained person, I am not afraid to discuss my NDE and also my subsequent visit with the Master to *anyone*. But please understand, because this experience is so sacred, I try not to "cast my pearls before the swine", as it were, for sometimes it just doesn't feel right and I will withhold. I'm sure there are some self-righteous Christians who look at this *entire* book as "...casting my pearls..." To them I say; "I am a witness that God lives – I **know** for I saw and talked with Him! I have been granted a special privilege to die and then to live again. I feel that were I *not* to share this, it would leave me embarrassed and guilty of ingratitude when I see Him again in the very near future. Also, you nay-Sayers don't have to believe *everything* that is put forth in this writing as doctrinally accurate, perhaps some is not completely correct (like I said, words can get in the way); but I tell you and you had *better believe;* that I saw my Savior Jesus Christ and that He lives and loves *all* of us!"

Anyway, like I said, I have talked with so many individuals on this side, which were grief stricken by the loss of a dear one and they have told me that they felt the presence of that person during a sacred time of meditation or grieving or during prayer. Some have even told me that they "smelled" them or sometimes felt them touch their side or shoulder or cheek. When they try to discuss this with other "living" family members or friends, they are often met with doubt or other forms of disbelief and cynicism. Unfortunately, we live in an extremely skeptical world today, when if so-called science cannot explain a phenomenon, then it cannot be true. Rubbish!

I tell them that our loved ones are not far from us. Indeed, they can see and hear, and *feel* what we feel. For them, the veil no longer exists. I will say that again. *For them, the veil no longer exists*. They are often frustrated by our bad habits or by some of the negative choices we make. Truly, many are given the *assignment* to watch over us, to protect us and to help us in whatever way they can. Our relationships with them are *eternal*.

I would like to explain a very important factor in our kinship with the dead. Because their spirits are so in-tune with our emotional state and well-being, the very powerful emotion of *grief* can be a hindrance to them – our grieving for them can actually *hold them back*. I've been with several friends and family who just simply, for whatever reason, "can't let go". You may be one of those individuals. Please understand this, I've felt and sometimes have seen those on the other-side disappointed, because all that intense mourning is *not allowing them* to move on! We need to remember that they are literally tied to us and we to them. Certainly *we* are not progressing when we are *consumed* with bereavement. It's also unfair for us, to not allow *their journey* to progress in the world of spirits, because of our prolonged remorse here on earth. Truly there is a time for mourning and then a time to move on. The quicker we accept this, the happier we will *all* be on both sides of the veil. This is not to say that our feeling of loss need ever go away, on the contrary, we need to remember and honor them and the lives they lived. But it is a matter of *focus and intensity*. Even for me, there is always a longing to be with them – a hole in my heart – until I'll be reunited with them permanently. We are after-all, eternal beings, therefore our relationships are eternal.

HOME & BACK AGAIN

Mama Passes-On

Because of the time difference between the Philippines and California; when we get a phone call at 3:00 AM, we know something serious is about to come down on us. A feeling of foreboding overcomes Tommy and I when the phone rings at zero-dark-early.

This time it was my wonderful niece (I have dozens) who was the bearer of bad tidings. "Mama Gurang is very sick... she is asking for you to come home now..."

I made my Mama promise me that she wouldn't pass-away until I saw her again. She was almost 92 years old when we got the message. I had just sold a house the week before, so we had the funds to get Ray and I there. This would be his first time going to the islands. Tommy had to work, so unfortunately he stayed behind.

Although I was so happy to be back home, the occasion for my being there was not a happy one – our great family matriarch was on her deathbed. Still, my nature is such that I tried to uplift all the other members of my family; siblings, aunts, uncles, and untold hundreds of nieces, nephews, cousins, and friends.

Raymond, then just ten years old, was treated like a "rock-star" by all his family, who just a few days before, had no idea of their existence. To say they spoiled him rotten is an understatement. However, for this I was grateful, because I was able to focus on Mama and the rest of the family's needs.

Because my status in the Philippines is "Fitness Queen" (whether deserved or not), my young nieces and their beautiful and equally young friends wanted me to show them how to "work-out". Although I was then and I still am, in pretty good shape, I am *not* young and as only the aged knows all too well, there is a huge difference! As timing would have it, we arrived during the start of the monsoon or as we Pinoys put it, "rainy season". Rain in the tropics must be experienced to be completely appreciated. "Rivers from the sky" is an adequate description. With all that rain comes mold, mildew, bacteria and bizarre strains of exotic sicknesses.

We had barely been in the country a few hours, it seems,

when these lovely Pinay's talked me into a workout. We had taken the bus down from Manila, which is *never* comfortable (our traveling companions usually include a few chickens, pigs and the occasional goat); this along with jet lag had me totally beat. It was brutally hot and exceedingly humid during our stay there. But who could resist all that exuberant, youthful energy?

Among other things, we did several sets of "guy" push-ups on the wet grass. That of course meant we had our noses in a "petri dish" of who-knows-what, while my already vulnerable body breathed in a laboratory of now foreign germs (30 years ago my body would have dealt with it). My now American immunity system (read weak) was already on the brink, when these brown beauties decided our workout included running up a local mountain road in the scorching humidity! The resulting Scarlet Fever nearly kept me from returning back to the U.S. (the S.A.R.S. scare was in full-steam). The malady permanently took much of my hearing in my left ear and lost me 15 pounds of muscle. "No good deed shall go..."

Aside from all that, I was able to spend two weeks with my mother and siblings. As mentioned before, most people in the Philippines are allowed to die, with dignity and peace at home.

We all took turns holding Mama and spending what we knew would be our last moments with her in this sphere. Because we were at home and there was no hospital staff telling us what we could and couldn't do while trying to prolong the inevitable, our time together was not stressful, harried or unpleasant.

The day before she passed, during one of my times taking care of Mama, although she was outwardly comatose; I continued to talk to her, knowing she was "in and out" as I had been so many times. During the course of our time together, sensing my father's presence, I asked her if Papa was there to pick her up. Immediately, she looked up and said, "Oh yes, he's right there smiling at me."

"Describe him for me Mama..."

"He's right there." Looking over my shoulder. "He looks so happy..."

"Are you ready to go with him?"

A brief pause... "...Yes, I'm ready..."

"Then, go with him Mama."

"Not yet, but soon..."

The next morning my oldest sister Fe was with her, when she called to us, "Something is wrong with Mama".

I came in and took her in my arms and gently caressed her cold skin and face. She was struggling to breathe; I suppose this is what is known as "death-rattle". I looked at her and asked her if she's saying "goodbye". Suddenly, her eyes opened and riveted on mine. They were clear blue (her normal eye color is brown, almost black) and they penetrated me with tranquility and peace, deep into my soul. She closed her eyes. I called the family in, and then I stepped out into another room where I knelt and prayed. I thanked Father in Heaven for my mother's peaceful passing and I asked Him if it would be possible that I could see Papa pick up Mama to take her home.

He granted me this wonderful vision, as I saw two beautiful spirits. They were both radiating golden light, dressed in the most exquisite white clothing. They were holding hands while walking away from me up in the "air".

A Few Nieces and Nephews At Mama's Funeral

IMELDA LORAYNA FOWLER

Mama & Papa 1984

Is this presumption Lord,
to ask that we be spared the role of slaves to death,
and that our sacrifices,
even as your own,
may build the road to life?

--- Louise H. Toness

Chapter 10

Healing Hands And Hearts

I don't remember exactly when I noticed I was given a very sacred gift of healing the sick and afflicted. Although I had always sought to give peace and comfort, particularly to the elderly, the acuity of this desire didn't peak until after I had died. All of us have been to doctors or physicians, but few of us have been to "healers". Granted, there are a few "professional" health care givers who do posses the gift of healing, but many rely too much on their clinical training to become truly effective healers.

In the Philippines we have a strange group of "espiritistas" or "spiritualists", also known as "faith healers". I'm not sure if many of them aren't just frauds who delight in taking unsuspecting foreigner's money while they "perform" their "miracles" to the enchantment of large audiences. If indeed, they are "healers", I don't think the Lord would be too pleased with how they *minister* their sacred gifts.

For me, the gift manifests itself in more subtle ways. Although I don't consciously seek out those in need, I am often guided to them by what appears on the outside to be simple happenstance. I've had so many instances where I *just happen* to be "in the right place" when I will see a stranger and I can discern through the Spirit, that they are "hurting". I am *not afraid* to speak

109

to anyone whom the Lord has led me to. So I'll usually initiate a conversation.

"Hello, how are you today? That's sure a pretty dress you have on..."

"Well, I'm not feeling very well today." Is the often weak or despondent response.

"Why? Is there anything I can do to help?"

"Thank you, but I really doubt there is anything you could do..."

Somehow, generally after a few disarming words and some heart felt smiles, I'm allowed "in". Usually the pain my new friend is experiencing is emotional (spiritual). Many have lost a loved-one to some sort of tragedy (*all death* can be a tragedy to those on this side of the veil). Most are on the verge of "giving up" and "don't know what to do". Others are hurting physically with some sort of painful ailment.

Although, I've been blessed to have helped many new friends (and old) through a spiritual crisis' and particularly bereavement, it is the last group I want to talk about here – those with physical ailments.

Massage is becoming a "re-discovered" way of promoting healing and revitalizing vigor and health. Most of us have had some form of massage by various professional or family members. Occasionally, we get "lucky" and find a person who possesses the gift of healing hands.

My gift was revealed to me gradually as I tried to help family members and old friends with various ailments. I was never trained in the "art" of massage, but somehow, instinctively, I know where the pain is. Even more importantly though, once I found the offending muscle spasm or painful knot, the touch of my hands seem to help alleviate the pain. Not in a magical or slight-of-hand way, but rather there is a powerful energy that seems to surge from my body (spirit) into the pain filled area. I can't explain it, but time and time again, tormented people will tell me that they've tried "everything" and the light massage I provided took the pain away.

Just one short example; we have a wonderful friend where we live. Val is well into her 90's (she won't tell anyone exactly how old she really is) and over the years we've become good friends. One day while talking to her, I noticed she was wincing in pain occasionally, by a few simple movements she made during our exchange. When I asked her why, she said she was having severe muscle problems in her arm and that she had been to doctors and specialists, but nothing seemed to help. "Can I have a look..." is my general response.

It was obvious where her problems stemmed from. Bless her heart, I could see a massive bulge in her tiny forearm and bicep; both were very tender and sore just to touch. I asked her if I could lightly massage her arm. She was a little hesitant, after all, she'd been to "specialists" and all they could do is prescribe painkillers for her, which she refused to take (perhaps that's why she's lived such a long and productive life?). She reluctantly held out her arm while I gently caressed her swollen muscles. Almost immediately she exclaimed with heartfelt relief, "I can't believe it! You've been able to take away the pain in just a few seconds... How did you do that? Did you know you had this gift?"

I was able to tell her about my NDE and how this seems to be something I was able to "take back with me". Now nearly every time I see her, I'm able to give her a little "rubdown" to take away some pain here and there.

Val is just one of many friends and strangers, whom I've been able to help. I thank the Lord for this precious gift He's given me. There are other gifts as well, including the special gift of *faith in prayer.*

My family and I love to go on extensive hikes and other outdoor activities. On one occasion, we took a wonderful hike in Northern California's Caribou Wilderness. Although the hike is not a particularly difficult one, Tommy was a little "soft" having worked the previous two years sitting at a desk (read computer nerd). We spent several days hiking, camping, fishing and just enjoying nature and each other. On the third night, when a black bear came passing through our camp, Tommy jumped up and began what he calls his "bear dance" (yelling, pounding pots, jumping and generally making a fool of himself – thankfully, for the most part, California bears are pretty passive – don't ever try a "bear dance" on a grizzly or Alaskan brown bear!). After his "Dances With Bears", Tommy immediately seized-up in a ball of cramps! He couldn't move, for when he went to stretch out one cramp, another would grab the next muscle group he was trying to straighten-out. He lay there in contorted agony, completely immobile.

I immediately called upon the power of silent prayer to help my poor husband be healed and released from this misery. Within a few seconds of my prayer, I heard him breathe a huge sigh of relief, as the power of the Lord washed over his distorted body. After a minute or two, he whispered to me,

"You said a prayer for me, didn't you? I knew you had, because nothing but the power of the Lord could have taken away the pain so quickly and completely…"

I have absolute faith in the Lord's healing power and in the power of prayer. There are countless other examples of personal healings and prayers, but they are personal and I don't wish to share them here.

I believe the *gift of service* is one of the grandest gifts we could not only possess but also exercise. The Savior was the greatest example of service to others; indeed, He spent His entire life giving, so others will prosper. Unfortunately, our society looks at giving money (tithing or other alms) as being equal with service. Nothing could be further from the truth. Although there is nothing wrong with offering alms (in any form), it is the giving of our time – *the most valuable commodity we possess* – that has lasting, eternal value. *Our greatest resource is ourselves.* When we give of that resource, we are offering something unique that nobody else on earth could offer.

I know I'm odd and might be called fanatical by some, but I

actually look for ways to serve others and then I *go out of my way* to seek out that individual. I pray every morning that the Lord will guide me to someone that I can give of myself to (and He does!). I find it interesting that we Christians profess our discipleship (root word – discipline) in the Master, but the minute something becomes a "burden" for us or our family or our *lifestyle,* we just "blow it off" and make lame excuses for our lack of commitment. Remember, this life is a testing ground. We will have to account for our lack of commitment when we saw an opportunity and let it pass us by; because perhaps it made us or our spouse feel "uncomfortable".

I love the story of the "Good Samaritan". We all know it, don't we? In a paraphrased nut-shell;

A man, a stranger, fell among thieves who beat him and robbed him of all his goods and then left him for dead. A few wealthy members of the religious ruling class (all of who *profess* their "love and *devotion* to God") came by him and saw him lying on the side of the road. Each of them walked around this poor fellow, each of them had a lame excuse for not taking of their time and means to help.

A lowly Samaritan (they were despised by the Jews of their day – lower than dogs), saw him and bound up his wounds, put him on his donkey (his Cadillac) and then took him to an Inn where he paid his room and board until he recovered and beyond.

Now, that's what I call commitment to serving our fellow man! He gave not only of his means (money – a large portion), but more importantly, he gave of his time. He didn't wait for the government to do something; he took that responsibility upon himself. I'm sure he wasn't completely "comfortable" with the situation and felt way-out of his "comfort zone". Still, he did *what was necessary* to help the stranger.

What a wonderful parable! There is something there that all of us could learn and grow from. The Lord expects us to leave our comfort zone and go and do good to our fellow beings. Again, I'm so grateful that I will *have to account* for all the good deeds I try to do everyday (I hope they "cover" my many sins)! It could be as simple as cheerfully saying "hello" to everyone (strangers) you meet. Tommy and I do it everywhere we go and the fruits are wonderful. Yes, we get "blown-off" sometimes, but you'd be pleasantly surprised at the positive results that come back to you when you make the effort to "brighten someone's day" with a cheerful "good morning".

The Most Powerful Force In The Universe

As we've already talked about, prayer is probably the most powerful tool we can use in our everyday life. Unfortunately that power lies dormant in most of us. Also, many who do pray regularly simply go through the *motions* of prayer and their offerings to the Lord can be anemic and weak. We need to train ourselves *and then train others*, how to offer heartfelt, powerful, and faith-filled prayers to the Master. I believe that *all sincere* prayers are answered, sooner or later. But I also believe and have seen, that there is a difference in how the Lord will accept and grant the petition of a concerned mother's prayer for her child, before He would accept a less than heartfelt offering from a frustrated student trying to pass an exam after partying all night. Although both have access to the same Light and Supremacy, it is the *motive* or *desire* that separates the two. We have all been on both sides of weak or powerful prayers, in one-way or another.

Like a muscle, prayer and faith need to be exercised regularly or they will atrophy and shrivel-up. Prayers used *only* during a crisis are not really prayers of faith at all, but rather they are desperate attempts of frustration and dissatisfaction or they become selfish complaints that things just aren't going our way.

When we pray often and believe with faith, that the Lord is hearing our pleas and more importantly our *thanksgiving* for blessings already received, our faith increases to the point where we are actually *looking to see* "small" miracles in our lives. Seeing those *daily* miracles take place increases our faith and strengthens our relationship with Deity. Then, in times of *real* crisis, we can turn to the Lord in powerful faith and KNOW that He is near *us* and

KNOW that He will *accept* our prayers and that *we* will *accept* whatever *His will is*, in humility. You may want to read that last sentence again, there's a lot of "meat" there.

I always end my prayers with a heart felt, THY WILL BE DONE… and I *mean* it! Saying and meaning those four words puts our lives into a whole new perspective and outlook. We are acknowledging that, in faith, we believe our God is in control and that *when we do the best we can*, we will accept the outcome – no matter what. This is faith in "Thy will be done".

Sometimes it's not just His will, that people can struggle with, but many times it is His *timing* that can be hard to accept. Therefore, our prayers not only need to include "Thy will be done", but *"Thy timing* be done" also. This can be a huge leap of faith! There are simply times when the Master wants us to wait, for whatever reason, to receive that blessing we seek so earnestly for (when we "die" and we have our "Life's Review", we'll look on that moment and say "Oh, so that's why…").

There are no *magic words* to prayer. There is no special place (like a church) that is only acceptable to offer prayers. Prayers of the heart can be offered in your car while driving (just don't close your eyes and bow your head!) or in a classroom before that big test (make sure you do *your part* by studying and making effort!). The Lord is God; therefore He is omnipresent (He is everywhere). For truly deep "groanings" in prayer, I like to have a special place (Tommy calls his place his "power spot"), where I can pour out my soul's desire to the Savior, study the word of God or I can just sit and ponder (meditate) on events or personal happenings. For me that place is on our boat's bowsprit (the long front of an old sailing ship, like ours). Daily meditation is absolutely essential to the inner-peace that is so elusive today. Scripture study is of utmost importance. I believe that the solution to every problem, no matter what, can be remedied in studying the Word of God.

So how does one pray? What are the mechanics? There is no one-way to pray, but I will humbly offer a way in which you, if you haven't already been taught how, can access the most powerful force in the universe, our Father in Heaven through His Son, Jesus

Christ. Here are my basic steps to prayer.

I begin by addressing He to whom I am speaking:

MY HEAVENLY FATHER...

Then I thank Him for all that I am grateful for. Sometimes that list never ends!

I THANK THEE (YOU) FOR...

Then I ask Him for what it is I seek (sometimes I don't ask Him for anything, I just want to thank Him and talk to Him).

I ASK THEE (YOU) FOR...

When I am finished talking to God, I close my prayers in the sacred name of His Son, Jesus.

I THANK THEE (YOU) AND ASK THEE (YOU) FOR THESE THINGS IN THE NAME OF JESUS CHRIST. AMEN.

I close my prayers this way because Jesus is our "advocate" with the Father. All things were created by Him (Jesus), He is our greatest supporter, and it is He who pleads our case before the Father. It is He who took upon Himself *our sins* in order for us to return back home in purity and righteousness.

Closing our prayers using "Amen" is like putting a formal, humble, exclamation point on the end of our heart felt supplication.

You will notice when I pray I use formal or "Old English" (Thee, Thy, Thou). I do so because I like my prayers to be special, and I try to use "special language" as it were – although doing so is not an absolute – after all, Father hears and answers the simplest prayers prayed by mere children. The words we use aren't nearly as important as the faith and desire we manifest in our spiritual supplication. However, I *never* approach Deity casually or in an informal way. Even though they are our best friends, they are still God…

I *know* THEY LIVE! I have seen them. I have stood before them. I have talked with them. I have literally been in the arms of my Lord Jesus Christ! I don't say that in pride or arrogance – it is simply a fact. Jesus is our best friend. Our Father in Heaven loves us. He loves us enough *not to* intervene sometimes in our lives that we may grow from our trials and hardships. Because they know *all things*, they know what is best for us, in every instance.

I've written this book because I've felt compelled by the Spirit to do so. Please don't discard the whole thing because you don't agree with *everything* in it. Certainly I am not perfect and more certainly, my opinions are not always correct.

Still, I hope you will take the good you find in here and *add it to what goodness is already in your heart*. I hope your faith in God has been lifted and your love for Him has grown through your reading this. If this is the case, then you have fulfilled my goal when I set out to humbly tell you of my incredible journey to the other side.

Thank you. I love you.

Medy Fowler

God is "AWESOME!"

IMELDA   LORAYNA   FOWLER

Raymond (12), Medy, Tommy

Back Into Competition

IMELDA   LORAYNA   FOWLER

What will the stars remember
After the earth is gone,
What dreams will they carry with them
Into a nobler dawn?

A man who flung, unflinching,
A truth against a lie,
A dog at the grave of his master,
And a cross against the sky.

--- Lilith Lorraine

Made in the USA
San Bernardino, CA
09 November 2013